Also by Linda Watson

The Ladies of Low Arvie

LIFE WITH THE LADIES OF LOW ARVIE

Continuing the Farming Dream

Linda Watson

iUniverse, Inc.
New York   Bloomington

Life with the Ladies of Low Arvie
Continuing the Farming Dream

Cover: Low Arvie Farmhouse 2009, Linda, Richard, Beauty

iUniverse books may be ordered through booksellers or by contacting:

iUniverse
1663 Liberty Drive
Bloomington, IN 47403
www.iuniverse.com
1-800-Authors (1-800-288-4677)

ISBN: 978-1-4502-2069-9 (pbk)
ISBN: 978-1-4502-2070-5 (ebk)

Printed in the United States of America

iUniverse rev. date: 3/18/2010

Acknowledgments

Thanks to George Carrick, photographer, Carlisle, for
kind permission to use some of his photographs.
Thanks, also, to Zvonco Cracun, photographer, Dumfries,
for creation of the cover from George's photographs.

For Richard and Catherine
And
In Memory of My Mother

Contents

Introduction

Low Arvie, January 2010

Hello again,

'Life with The Ladies of Low Arvie' continues our story begun in my first book 'The Ladies of Low Arvie' in which I catalogued the many trials that we faced after the purchase of Low Arvie, our small farm in Dumfries and Galloway, SW Scotland. 'The Ladies of Low Arvie' ended with the successful birth of our first batch of home bred calves and the end to many of our problems with the completion of our house extension, the bringing of mains water to our property and our learning of the rules and regulations to which farming in the 21st Century is subject.

We thought that we had faced and overcome most of the challenges that buying Low Arvie would bring us and that life would continue on in unremarkable fashion from that point. Little did we know what the future held for us as we settled into our new life with 'The Ladies' and their new offspring.

My mother, too, had settled into her new home close by in Castle Douglas and was forming new friendships and finding new activities in this the latter portion of her life.

I always answered the readers of my first book who asked for more in the same way. Surely there could not be anything else of interest that would happen to us and our small, but beautiful, homestead that would justify my taking to the typewriter again.

This book is a testament to just how wrong I was!!

I have attempted to include just enough of the previous story to allow those who have not read that to follow the narrative, but, hopefully, not enough to allow previous readers to become bored. I have also included parts of those first years that were not included the first time around in order to complete the record of our journey so far.

In spite of, and because of, all that life at Low Arvie has been, we are continuing to live our dream and to gain true satisfaction from doing so. Overcoming each fresh challenge adds to our enjoyment and I hope that reading this next instalment of our story adds to yours!

I

Low Arvie

The first two years of our occupation at Low Arvie had been hectic and exhilarating. We had arrived to take possession on July 11th 2002 with no farming equipment and little idea of what we were to do and in the following months we had set up a beef rearing enterprise. The land was very wet and the six years of neglect since the previous farmer had died had left the fields and tracks in a very sorry state. Our first job had been to get the grass cut and made into silage and achieving this process in the first two weeks of our occupation had improved the look of the place considerably. But this only dealt with 20 of the 120 acres and the remaining rough grazing land was brought somewhat back into shape by the cattle of two of the farmers who had helped us make our silage. This left the tracks to be dealt with and this was a problem not so easily solved and for the first months we were in residence I had only been able to walk on the land in the very driest time because, as soon as the rain came, huge areas of the tracks became deep pools of almost liquid mud and were dangerous to man and beast. The remedying of these took time and money and tons and tons of rock quarried from the land of another neighbour. Eventually though Low Arvie began to take on a cared-for look and an air of respectability.

We bought our own herd of pedigree Black Galloways, who have become the Ladies of Low Arvie, from a local estate that was being sold up and they were delivered one exciting day in November in three livestock lorries. The twenty four cows had brought with them eighteen calves, six bull calves and twelve heifers. One of the bulls had tragically died but the remaining seventeen had grown and flourished in our large cattle shed until we had been able to drain the land sufficiently for them to take their rightful place in the fields. The five now castrated bullocks had grown into fine beasts on the land of another farmer, Graham, who has become a close friend. They were to fulfil their fate in the summer of 2004, giving a welcome boost to our severely depleted finances. The destiny of the twelve heifers was to become suckler cows to provide more calves and we put them out into the field at the far end of the farm to grow. They would be ready to make their first encounter with the bull in the summer of 2004, producing their first calf in late spring 2005.

The older Ladies themselves, now reduced to twenty-two in number by the loss of one who was ill when she came and a second one who was unable to breed, had braved the wet land and, happily, were used to finding their way around very wet spots, as their previous home on Bardennoch Hill had been in very similar conditions. They met successfully with the bull, Zeppelin, hired from Gordon Gilligan at High Creoch, Gatehouse of Fleet, and had all produced our first batch of home bred calves in the autumn and winter of 2003/4. We had made our second crop of silage with the help of kind neighbours and the hindrance of poor second hand machinery and had overcome the challenges we had faced with fortitude on Richard's part and just the tiniest degree of panic (slight understatement) on mine!

Once our first calves were born and doing well, we hired Zeppelin once again. He was a gentle giant, hand reared by Gordon in the same way as we rear ours and we gladly welcomed him back to Low Arvie where he obligingly created our second crop of calves. There were only sixteen this time as some of the cows were getting quite old and their breeding life was coming to an end. We took stock of the herd and decided to part with four of these when their first calves were weaned. The land was still not in good heart and now that the older calves that had come with the cows were out of the shed where they had spent their first winter, we feared that the land would suffer badly if there were too many feet churning up the mud. It was a sad time taking the cows on their last journey but, in the same way as it is often kindest to put a beloved pet to sleep, so we felt about the old cows. Because they live most of their lives out in the weather and would not take kindly to being shut up in sheds at any time, they are inclined to arthritis in the latter stages if their lives (who isn't?) and it would not be fair to expect them to carry embryonic calves who weigh up to 45 kilos at birth, when their hips and backs are causing them pain. The remaining two that were not in calf to Zeppelin seemed to be still in good health and we decided to keep these and, when the Bardennoch Hill calves were ready to be served in the late summer of 2004, we put these two cows with them

We then had to decide what to do with the first batch of Low Arvie calves, who were by now almost a year old. The winter was fast approaching and the autumn rain was falling with increasing frequency and it was clear that we needed to reduce the numbers before the winter came. There was the annual sale of Galloways in the market in Castle Douglas at the end of October and we thought about sending them there to be sold. However, although we do go to the market and know that the animals are not treated badly, I was not keen to subject our calves to the noise and bustle, and to being poked and prodded around the ring whilst the auctioneer loudly proclaimed the bids. We had fourteen bullocks and eight heifers and they had all grown well and were making good beasts. We talked several times about our options and then worried quietly about what to do. The solution came, as usual for us, from an unexpected source. While we were seeking a bull to run with the Bardennoch Hill heifers, we were advised by Margaret in the Galloway Society office to get in touch with John Finlay. John lives at Blackcraig Farm about five miles from Low Arvie and he farms it with the help of his wife, Ann, and son, Ian. They are very well known in the world of Black Galloways and Blackcraig animals often win prizes and fetch the highest prices in the mart. We were assured that John would know of anyone with a spare bull for hire and so I rang him and told him of our need. During the course of the conversation he mentioned that he had seen our animals as he drove past Low Arvie on his way to Castle Douglas and he thought they looked good. He told us that the MacMillans at Overbarskeoch may be able to help in the question of the bull and then went on to enquire if we were thinking of selling any of our stock. He said that he knew of someone who was wanting to buy Galloway bullock calves and he said we would get a fair price. This seemed to be ideal and we arranged for him to come with his friend to look at our boys.

We also followed up on John's suggestion for a bull and I rang Alan McMillan. He said they had two possibilities. Both were young bulls, untried in the field, and Richard went to 'interview' them. He decided that Lucky Strike would be fine and Alan brought him to Low Arvie to join our 'girls'. We hoped that the vigour of youth and the beauty of our heifers would inspire him to the required action! It did and he got all but three of the heifers and both old cows in calf. These two old cows were Gladeye, mother of Low Arvie calf number 2, named Lucky, who had spent his first hours of life in the cold water of the main farm ditch, and Diana, mother of Wee Boy who had also given us some anxiety and had been nursed through his early days in the old shed.

A few days later John arrived with Ian and Scott McKinnon and they went off with Richard to see the yearling calves, which we had shut in the shed for convenience. They seemed to like what they saw and shortly Richard brought the men into the kitchen for tea and cake and to fix a price. Scott is the farm manager of a large holding near Moniaive, a small village about twenty miles from Corsock and, as well as owning the holding, his boss has several garden centres throughout England and Scotland. He was gradually putting farm shops into these and wished to sell only Galloway beef in them. Scott had about thirty Galloway suckler cows, but the holding he managed held mostly commercial beef breeds. He had been charged to build up his stock of Galloways to service the garden centres but in the meantime he needed to outsource calves to fatten. He was very pleased to buy our fourteen and, as John had foretold, he offered a good price and agreed to come and fetch the animals the next week. This was very pleasing to me because the animals would be taken straight from our fields to Scott's farm and would suffer very little stress in the process. As we drank our tea and talked, we mentioned that we needed to sell some of the young heifers as well and to our surprise, John said that he would buy as many as we wanted to sell. Once again we found our path opening before us and we said we would sort out how many we wanted to sell and get in touch with him soon.

As we were losing four of the old cows, we decided to keep three of the heifers as replacements and Richard allowed me to choose them. I found it quite difficult as I knew them all and this was my first taste of putting head before heart, in recognising that we were running a business instead of looking after sixty pets. The very favourite amongst the old cows is Beauty. Although the youngest of them, she has somehow become the leader of the pack and will come to my call, bringing the rest of the herd with her. This is very useful when we want to feed them or move them to new grazing. Her calf had inherited her strong formation and the proud carriage of her head which, because it is always held a little higher than the others, allows us to pick her out of the crowd. I therefore put her calf, number 10, Lady Olga, on top of the 'keeping list'.

The day that Alex MacDonald had come out from the Galloway Society to help us name and register the Bardennoch Hill calves shortly after their arrival, he had looked over the herd and picked out two or three cows that he thought might win prizes if ever we went into showing. The best one of these was Zinnia and her first Low Arvie calf had been number 11, a heifer that we had called Lady Pete. This might appear a strange name for a female, but she was named for Richard's mother who had never grown taller than 4 feet 10 and a half (never forget the half) inches and so was always known as Peter Pan, or Pete for short. Lady Pete was second on my 'keeping list'.

The third place was more difficult to fill. I looked at the calves and looked at their history and could not find a reason to keep any particular one above the others as Alex's other choice cows had all had bull calves. I went outside to look at them grazing in the field and there was one that was smaller than the others and more nervous. I looked up her pedigree and found that she was Lady Rebecca (named for my daughter's best friend at school). She was the half sister of Lady Linda (no prizes for guessing where that name originated!). Lady Linda had come with her mother from Bardennoch Hill in the lorry and had been the youngest and smallest of her batch. However, she had grown into a fine heifer with a good conformation and now had the makings of an excellent cow. I looked at Rebecca and thought that she might do the same. I also hoped that she would lose her nervousness under Richard's gentle care and I added her name to my list. I then rang John and told him that we would keep three and sell him the remaining five, to which he agreed.

I was not quite correct in my surmising about Rebecca! She has remained the smallest cow we have and her calves are small too. She has never entirely lost her nervousness either. However what she lacks in size, she makes up for in fertility because she is usually the first to calve every year!

2

Aga blues

We had been at Low Arvie for twenty months when the birth of Lady Tracey had brought the first round of Low Arvie calves to its successful conclusion, and as winter had changed into spring we had watched them grow from the cute, black, perfect replicas of their mothers into the leggy ranginess of 'teenage' Galloway calves with their shaggy, untidy brown coats. Towards the end of their first year, this brownness would once more resolve itself into the jet blackness of adult Galloways.

Around the same time we had been able to move into the new extension which doubled the size of the original Galloway cottage that was the farm house. The weather was kinder than the previous year and we were very comfortable in the warmth of the new kitchen and bedroom. The builder, electrician and joiner had all worked together to finish off their various portions of the work in excellent fashion and the plumber was eventually prevailed upon to do his. He managed to complete with only a few disappointing errors. The one thing we did insist that he put right was the route of the hot water from the boiler in the Aga to the tank in the bathroom directly above and thence back to the sink in the kitchen below. For some reason he had sent the piping for the hot water right along the upstairs from the new bathroom through the old bedrooms to the far end of the house and then back along the same route to the new kitchen. It took all of three minutes for it to travel this distance and several gallons of cold water were wasted each time and the same amount of hot water remained in the pipes to go cold after each usage. We insisted that he changed this route and send the hot water directly down into the kitchen below.

The last job he had to do was to remove the bath in the old bathroom and replace it with a shower for the use of our Bed and Breakfast guests. He had promised to come several times and not appeared, giving no explanation for his absence, so that when he did eventually arrive, we left him to get on with the job in the hope that he would finish quickly and go. When he drove away and we went to inspect the shower, we were not surprised, but just sad, to find that he had erected it in the wrong corner of the room. Instead of it standing neatly by the washbasin where we intended, leaving a comfortable space by the door for a small cupboard with mirror above, there it was, cement setting nicely, in that very corner, leaving an awkward space between the shower cabinet and the wash basin. There were other things too, but we decided not to ask him to come and change either the shower or these other things, as we felt that we could not go through the agonising process of requesting him to come and then being disappointed again when he didn't, and we learned to live with these minor inconveniences.

However, that was not the last of the dealings we had with him. One stormy night in the late autumn, we were awoken to the sound of loud explosions taking place in the kitchen below us. Not only that, but on opening our eyes we became aware that each explosion was accompanied by a flash which was reflected up the open staircase onto the bedroom wall in front of us. Flames were shooting out of the Aga and licking at the old oak cupboard on the other side of the room. Our senses of smell and taste were also assailed by the unmistakable odour of kerosene which was slowly filling the house. Looking at the clock I saw that it was 1.30 a.m., and with fuddled brains unable to understand the 'son et lumiere' display that was going on down below, we rushed out of bed and hurried to see the intermittent flames shooting out of the Aga. Richard was the first to cotton on to the problem, and he explained that the wind, which was howling outside and quite audible between the explosions, was coming down the flue pipe and blowing the flame out between the grating bars in the tiny fire door of the Aga (along with plenty of oily, black soot which was being deposited around the kitchen) and then extinguishing it. The vapour then built up again and relit itself causing the explosive noise. We went to find the Aga instructions but could find nothing in them relevant to our situation and decided the only thing to do was to turn the kerosene off and let the Aga go out. By this time the house was filled with fumes and so we had to open all the windows in the kitchen and bedroom, which allowed all the built up heat to escape along with the fumes, making the house cold.

We spent the next morning cleaning up the mess and when the wind died down in the early afternoon, Richard set about re-lighting the Aga. We still had the original Esse range working in the old kitchen/office where we were able to cook and make drinks, so breakfast and lunch had not been too disrupted, but the new part of the house felt cold and we were anxious to return it to our comfort zone as quickly as possible. However, it soon became clear that the re-lighting process was not going to be as easy as hoped. As the cooker cooled down over the previous hours, the carbon in the oil jets had solidified and would not allow the oil to flow through them. It was a job for the experts! We spent some time locating our local chap, but eventually discovered that he is Michael Ross who lives about ten miles away, and we rang him. He was unable to come out that day, but agreed to come early the next morning.

He arrived promptly at 9.30 a.m. and proceeded to investigate the situation. We reported the happenings of two nights previously, and he went outside and peered upwards. 'There's your problem', he said, pointing up at the shiny flue that protruded from the new roof. 'You've got the wrong cowl – that one is for gas Agas, not kerosene. Furthermore I don't think the flue is high enough. It needs to be above the ridge line of the roof.' Yet one further problem created by the plumber! We set about finding an expert in Aga cowls, whilst Michael started to take the Aga apart and de-coke the working parts. With the wind no longer an issue, he soon had the stove re-lighted and the kitchen took on its accustomed air of warmth and comfort. Meanwhile, an exhaustive search of the Internet had provided the telephone number of a company in Manchester who dealt in cowls, and Richard spent half an hour on the telephone discussing our problem and possible solutions. Finally, following the advice of the very knowledgeable person on the other end of the phone, he agreed to purchase a new cowl which would hopefully solve the problem. The man in Manchester had heard of this happening before and could not guarantee that we would be trouble free in the future but he said things should be better with this different style. When the new cowl arrived, Richard climbed the ladder to the top of the roof and gingerly removed the old cowl and re-placed it with the new differently shaped one. The plumber was prevailed upon to come and take the old cowl away and refund the cost of it. Fortunately, he came when we were out and picked it up from the barn and sent the cheque through the post.

Unfortunately the problem was not solved entirely by the new cowl, and every time the wind blew exactly from the east (happily it did this only once or twice a year) we were subjected to the same explosive occurrence and we had to send for Michael to relight the Aga each time. The final time it happened was the spring bank holiday week end at the end of May 2008, when the wind blew from the relevant direction for three days and three nights. By this time we had grown used to the process and we turned the Aga off at the first sign of trouble and rang for Michael to come and clean it up the next day. The wind was still blowing fiercely that day and so he did not re-light the flame but left everything ready for Richard to do so when the wind died down. We had to wait two more days for this to happen, and the heart of our home lost all of its warmth and happy feeling and we were transported once more back to the 'bad old days' when the house felt colder inside than out. Happily this was May and the insulation throughout the new part of the house had some effect, but it was clear that something needed to be done to resolve the issue once and for all. The flue pipe was extended to lift it higher than the ridge as Michael had suggested on the first occasion and a third cowl was purchased. This one turns with the wind and so is always positioned correctly for the current air flow and hopefully, this minor but irritating inconvenience will finally be a thing of the past, not least because it has been an intermittent but constant reminder of the plumber!.

None of this has dulled my pleasure in owning my beautiful four-oven British racing green Aga. I have gradually gained in confidence when using it and can produce reasonable, edible cakes and have even progressed to offering evening meals to our Bed and Breakfast guests, something unthinkable just a few short years ago. Friends who have re-appeared in my life (owing to their discovery of my first book 'The Ladies of Low Arvie' and some detective work on the Internet) have been astonished at this addition to my portfolio of skills, having known only someone who previously never touched an oven or a saucepan in cold blood!

3

Open University

We had been looking for a farm for about three years before we found Low Arvie. During that time Richard had spent the summers working for the farmer in the village in South Yorkshire where we were living (where we had both been born and brought up and where we had got together in the second half of our lives). I was spending my time following counselling training at the local college. We began to spend the winter months holidaying and making plans for the future and when Richard went to work on the farm each May when the harvesting of the peas began, I turned my attention to our internet search for a suitable farm. Our mothers were both still alive and in their nineties and so the search was initially more in the nature of research rather than an active process. However, after the century turned, interest rates were dropping and the stock market where Richard's money was invested also began to look rocky and so we decided that the search was becoming more urgent. As the property purchasing process in Scotland is so uncertain with its closed bids system, we knew that it could be a long time before we were successful even if we found properties that were suitable, and so I continued my counselling training at the same time as continuing the search. The successful purchase of Low Arvie in July 2002, however, cut both of these occupations short and prevented me from taking the place I had gained at Strathclyde University to follow their Diploma in Counselling Course.

Once the farm was up and running, I decided to complete my counselling qualification and achieved a Diploma by doing an on-line course in 2003. Richard suggested that I follow this up by studying for a Bachelor level degree with the Open University. I have always felt that I could have achieved a degree, as did most other members of my family and I realised that this would be something that I could now prove. In October 2004, I therefore received a parcel of books and assignments and began the long journey to gaining a Bachelor of Science with Honours degree. On June 6th 2009 I was proud to be presented with an upper second class BSc Honours degree at the Royal Concert Hall in Glasgow. It has been a hard road at times but for the most part an enjoyable one and the good results I have achieved along the way have boosted my self confidence and the whole process has helped to heal long standing health problems, not to mention increasing my knowledge. Because I wanted to gain a Science degree, which most of the family have, I had obviously to follow a lot of Science courses, and with no Science education background, these were the most difficult for me.

The Open University degree course is based on a point system. You have to gain a minimum of 300 points, including at least 60 from the higher rated level 3 courses for an ordinary degree and a further 60 at level 3 to achieve a degree with Honours. The standard method is to gain 120 points from each of levels 1, 2 and 3 and this was my goal when I set out. For a Science degree I needed half or more of my points to come from Science and Science related courses and the rest could be made up from any other section of the prospectus. For my first course I chose the 60 point Discovering Science course. This consisted of twelve sections, each with their own text book and each covering a different facet of Science. The material covered everything from particles inside an atom to the furthest reaches of space and all things in between. Each section had a related assignment to test the knowledge gained and instead of a final examination there was a further assignment covering many aspects of the course. It began in October 2004 and ended nine months later. From the first day I opened Book 1, I was hooked on the fascinating world of knowledge that was opening up before me. I was quite ashamed of the great number of things that I didn't know and I read the books with mounting excitement and relished the challenge of the assignments as they came along.

I am aware that my personality is such that I usually take up new interests with great enthusiasm and then suffer burn out and begin to lose interest and so I decided to hurry the process of gaining a degree along as quickly as possible and, having got the Science course well under way between October and February, I registered to begin the 30 point level 1 Spanish course and a further short 10 point science course about Nutrition and Health. There was also a practical science course scheduled to take place in July 2005 at Heriot Watt University in Edinburgh, which would give me another 10 points, making 110 of my level 1 points achieved in the first year.

I made plans to go to Edinburgh for the practical course in the final week of its four week run for 2005 because by then the heifers should have given birth to their first calves and they would all be out at grass for the summer. This would enable Richard to take a well earned break and join me in Edinburgh for the week. His brother had agreed to come up and farm sit and we would leave him a list of useful telephone numbers, vet, helpful neighbours etc. for any emergencies.

The girls that had run with Lucky Strike were due to calve between May and early July and we had had them scanned for pregnancy and discovered that nine of the heifers and the two older cows were in calf. Of the remaining three heifers, one had received a bad injury and had to be put down, another, Lady Barbara, never did get in calf and was found to be deformed internally and the third, Lady Gina went on to get pregnant to Zeppelin the next autumn.

Lady Freya was the first to calve on May 12th and the other eight followed in the next days. The two older cows had not been put in with the bull until a few weeks after the heifers and they were still waiting for their calves as July began. Diana had her calf on July 6th but old Gladeye was still waiting as the day we were to leave for Edinburgh approached. It began to look as if Richard would have to stay at Low Arvie and await the birth while I went to Edinburgh alone, but then on the afternoon of July 22nd, we watched her proceed to her lonely spot and we knew that the birth was imminent. We have a bag in which we keep the equipment needed to deal with a new born calf, including a towel to rub warmth into the little body, the ear tags that have to be inserted in the ears and antiseptic to spray on the dangling umbilical cord through which a new calf can pick up infection. Richard picked up the bag and went off to try and tag the calf and make sure that all was well. The calf was born just as he arrived and he could see that the membrane which had protected the unborn calf appeared to be still wrapped around its face. He slowly approached near enough to remove the membrane but Gladeye did not appreciate that he was trying to help and, leaving the cattle cake that he had provided to divert her attention for a few minutes, she prepared to attack. Richard was just able to swipe the membranes away from the little face and retreat to a safe distance before Gladeye roared towards him. The episode set the scene and each time Richard attempted to get near enough to put the tag into the calf's ear, Gladeye made it clear that she was not going to allow it. In spite of his gentle blandishments to try and reassure her, she was intransigent, and, after three abortive attempts, Richard gave up and left her to clean the little fellow and get him suckling. They were down in the rushes in the Eastside field and when they were still there the next morning and the calf was on its feet and suckling, Richard decided that they were fine and he would come to Edinburgh and hope that Gladeye would be calm enough for him to tag the calf on our return a week later.

Richard's brother, John, arrived to take charge and we armed him with the list of telephone numbers should help be required. We warned him from approaching too near to Gladeye and said he should call Tom Corsan from Arvie farm, who, as an experienced cattle farmer, would know how to deal with Gladeye and the calf, if he was at all concerned.

With a tinge of anxiety we left for Edinburgh.

4
Yoghurt

All appeared to be well for the first few days of our absence, but on the Thursday John began to be concerned about Gladeye's calf. He did not seem to be suckling any more and was just lying miserably in the rushes. When things were no different on the Friday, he rang Tom and asked him to come and see what he thought. It was almost dark by the time Tom managed to come to Low Arvie and he, too, was concerned that all was not well with the calf. Gladeye must have realised that he needed help and without too much difficulty, John and Tom were able to get both cow and calf into the shed for the night and Tom said that he would return in the morning and do a closer inspection of the calf in the daylight.

The next day was Saturday and we returned home in the early afternoon to find a very sorry little calf lying in the shed. Tom had been in the morning and discovered that he had been attacked by flies whilst lying in the rushes and his whole body from just behind his front legs to his rear end was covered with hundreds of clusters of fly eggs. Just after we returned, Tom came back with a container of sheep dip and he and Richard spent an hour and a half treating the eggs with the dip and clipping away the infested hair from the calf's body. We decided to leave him and his mother in the shed and keep watch to see how things went. He certainly appeared more comfortable but we wanted to see him up on his feet and suckling well before letting them go.

Things did not take this happy turn and the next day he remained lying down. We became concerned that he was not suckling at all and so we took them across the yard to the old byre where there was a crush and Richard put Gladeye into the crush and milked her so that we could feed the calf with her milk from the bottle. He was not very interested in eating at all for two days but we persevered with milking Gladeye and forcing the life giving liquid into the calf. Richard also injected him with antibiotics to cope with any infection that he might have picked up. Although he did not appear to be dying, he spent most of his time lying in the straw and we could hear him grinding his teeth. At the end of the second day, we decided to call out the vet for help and advice.

The vet that came that day was not Roddy, our usual vet, but his colleague, John Sproat. He examined the calf and we told him of our observations about the teeth grinding. He said that this was indicative of pain and suggested that the antibiotic might have caused the calf's gut to stop working properly and he asked me if I had any yoghurt in the house. I happened to have a large tub of the natural biotic kind in the fridge and I went to fetch it. John took out a large needleless syringe from his car and filled it from the yoghurt pot. He squirted the whole syringe full into the calf's mouth and then gave him a second syringe full. He thought that the bacilli in the yoghurt might help to get the gut working again. He also gave the calf an injection of vitamins and told us to repeat the yoghurt treatment over the next days and try to get the calf suckling again.

We spent a long time trying to do this but Gladeye was not very cooperative and would not stand still to let Richard tempt the calf to her udder. She was very wild and it was a dangerous process to go into the byre unless she was restrained in the crush and, when she was in the crush, it was not possible to get the calf near to her udder. We continued to feed him the yoghurt and her milk from the bottle but we knew that this could only be a short term measure as he was losing the idea that the milk came from his mother and he began to look to me for his food instead of her. Richard rigged up a temporary crush that allowed better access to her udder but both mother and calf became stressed when we attempted to get him to suckle. Her teats had also become dry and cracked through not being sucked and were less appetising to the calf than the smooth artificial teat on the bottle. We struggled on for a day or two but seemed to be losing the battle. The calf was still grinding his teeth and showing little inclination to seek sustenance for himself. It was a fight to get him to take much of the milk at all and we began to feel desperation.

On the third day Richard had an inspiration and we let the calf get as hungry as possible and then we restrained Gladeye in the temporary crush and smeared double cream over her teats and gave the calf a taste of it too. When we brought him near to his mother the next time he found the cream on her teats and, miraculously, began to suckle. Each day we kept watch to see if he would go and suckle from her voluntarily and when he didn't, we repeated the process with the cream. Each time he seemed to take more interest in the process and suckled successfully, but we still had to manoeuvre Gladeye into the crush and push the calf under her rear end to her udder. Then, about the fourth day, when we went to the byre to feed him, we were rewarded with the sight of him standing on his feet suckling for himself without our aid and we breathed a huge sigh of relief.

However, he still seemed lethargic and lacked the joie de vivre that the young calves usually show. We remembered how Wee Boy had raced round and round the shed after a few days of confinement there with his mother, when we had been concerned for his health following his birth, but this calf, now named Yoghurt, did not show any inclination to do anything other than lie in the straw, only occasionally getting up and walking dejectedly around. However, now that he was suckling, we were more hopeful of his survival.

When it seemed that we could do no more for him, we opened up the shed and let the mother and calf out into the field with the rest of the herd. They were all in the fields closest to the house and it would be easy to keep Yoghurt under surveillance and we hoped that the fresh air and the company of the other calves would encourage him to become more lively.

Three or four days later I went down to open the gate into the next field to give the herd a fresh supply of grass and I stood at the gate as Beauty led them through, eager to eat the juicy grass that she could see there. As Yoghurt passed me I looked carefully at him and was horrified to see that a large open sore had suddenly appeared at one side of his tail head. Quickly I found Richard and fetched him to see. The month was now August when the flies were at their worst and we could plainly see several buzzing around the sore and crawling over it. There was only one thing to do and that was to get him and his mother back to the safety of the shed where we could minister to him once more. The sore was quite large, covering about four square inches and when we had finally got them into the shed, we could see that there was another smaller sore opening up at the other side of his back. Fortunately we had some antibiotic powder in the medicine cabinet and this seemed to be the most appropriate treatment for the sores. Gladeye was still uncooperative, perhaps even more so now that she found herself once more confined in the shed. She would try to attack whenever Richard went into the shed and so, each time we wanted to administer the powder, she had to be restrained in the crush first. This process was quite dangerous and required Richard to be very careful not to get in her way and he always kept the gates, with which we could partition the shed into three pens, between him and her. All this took a considerable amount of time because, when the powder was absorbed into the wound, it became open and bloody and the flies would start to land on it again. The only thing to do was to keep it covered as much as we could with the powder and this meant applying it several times each day.

Two days later a huge piece of skin and hair lifted away near the smaller sore making this wound even larger than the first one. We realised that this had been the cause of his lethargy and teeth grinding as he must have been in a lot of pain and we could only think that the sheep dip that Tom and Richard had used to remove the fly eggs had been so caustic that it had burnt his young skin. As the wounds were raw and deep, we knew that they would take a long time to heal and that Gladeye and Yoghurt would have to stay in the shed until this had happened. Apart from the time it took each day to dress the wounds, it was also inconvenient because Gladeye had to be fed in the trough as she could not eat the grass in the fields with the other cows. We sourced some bales of hay from a farmer friend who always seems to be able to help out with feed and straw, and the two remained in the shed for the two months that it took for Yoghurt to be returned to full health. Eventually the sores did heal and the hair grew back from the new skin, although the hair that grew was a much lighter colour and finer than the rest.

At the beginning of October we were able to allow them back into the fields with the rest of the herd, but Yoghurt, by now almost three months old, did not seem able to socialize with the other calves, having spent so long with just his mother for company, and whenever we saw him, he was always on his own wandering around whilst the others played their galloping games around the fields.

None of the farmers we told this story to had ever heard of a calf being subjected to fly strike as Yoghurt had been, but apparently it was quite common for it to happen to lambs and our neighbour, Dorothy, told us that the answer was to wash the affected animal down with a simple solution of washing up liquid. I hope it never happens again but, if it does then we will certainly try this remedy and hope for less dramatic results!

5

'The Ladies of Low Arvie'

Buying the farm and moving to Scotland had been the most exciting event in my life, with the exception of giving birth to my daughter, Catherine. I had spent all my life in the same South Yorkshire village, only leaving briefly in the sixties to go to Teacher Training College in Derby, and I suppose I expected to remain there. When Richard had decided that he wanted to buy a farm, he also said that he wanted it to be in a more quiet location away from the hurly burly of life in Yorkshire, and so we began to search northwards, eventually buying Low Arvie in Dumfries and Galloway. Richard had spent all his adult life in one form of agriculture or another, beginning work on a farm at the age of sixteen, and progressing through day release classes to gain City and Guild qualifications and doing 'A' levels at the local Technical College. He then gained a place to do a degree at Aberystwyth University and, after a two year stint teaching the natives of Ecuador how to store potatoes, he had gone on to have successful career as a lecturer in Agricultural Colleges. He had never, though, had any direct experience of farming suckler cows and we were learning this process together. We were therefore very pleased with our efforts at turning Low Arvie from the rather sad and forlorn little farm into a successful venture and enjoyed the sight of our own cows and calves roaming the improved pasture that we had created.

I have never kept a diary, but I felt that this monumental stage of my life was worth recording and in spare moments during our first year, I would sit at the computer and write about the experience. It soon became apparent that each time I wrote it turned into a chapter length 'essay'. However, there were no thoughts at all in my head of it ever becoming a book, just a record to enable Richard and me to look back on and remember our adventure when we got old and the farm was a thing of the past.

This changed because the Open University provides internet 'chat rooms' where communication can take place between students. This is helpful because there is not much chance to meet up with fellow students face to face and studying at home can be a lonely process. When I began the first Science course, I found my way around the OU website and soon became a regular visitor to the 'chat room' for my course. Here we could help each other with queries about the course or just post interesting, relevant messages, although we were not allowed to ask or answer direct questions about the assessments which would form part of our course marks. On this forum, I had 'met' a lady in my own age bracket who was setting out on the same process of gaining a degree and we became internet friends and, after exchanging our normal email addresses, we began a daily exchange of messages outside the OU room, in which we could discuss personal details and more general information. I began to include snippets of information about the farm in these messages: what Richard was doing, when the vet came, what was happening to the cows etc. and she always showed great interest in these. She lives in Somerset near the countryside but has little actual knowledge of the world of farming and she began to ask me questions about our life. One day, without referring to it directly in my daily email, I attached the first 'chapter' of my writing about buying the farm and clicked on the send button. The next day I received her response which was quite amazing to me. 'Well, come on, then', she wrote, 'where's the rest. You can't leave me with just this bit. I need to know what happened next.' And so every day I would attach the next portion of our story to my mail and she told me that she would print it off and read it as recreation from her studies with her morning coffee. At this stage I had only completed about twenty days worth of reading and so, in between all my other work, I began to write more chapters to send to her. Slowly the story grew, telling in detail how we began our venture, how we bought the cows, the problems we had with cold and water, the worries I had about my mother and how they were solved, how we learned to cope with the EU rules which didn't fit in with either our land or our climate and, of course, the happy ending of the birth of our first calves. That seemed to be a natural ending to the story and I informed her that she would have to find other reading matter for her coffee break.

Her response to this last chapter astounded me. 'I didn't tell you before,' she wrote, 'but before I retired I worked as a proof reader. I have read many books and I think your story would make an excellent book. It is interesting, full of information which is not generally known and, also, has made me laugh out loud several times. I think you should see about getting it published.' To say I was flabbergasted at this is a great understatement, but remembering all the hours I had spent at the computer and buoyed up by her kind words, I set about finding the address of a publisher. Never one to like putting my head above the parapet very much, I found this whole thing to be quite a difficult concept. I worried that I had named so many people in our story and wondered what they would think to see themselves in print. I read each piece through carefully and discovered that I had only been complementary to these people. I could hardly have done anything else, as most of them had been so kind to us and the few that hadn't weren't named at all. I searched our Yellow Pages directory for a local publisher, but could not find one and googling 'Publishers in Dumfries and Galloway' produced no results either and so I found the address of Michael Joseph who had published the James Herriot books and sent them several of the chapters. I sat back and waited for their rejection slip to arrive. When it came, it said that they could not use the book, but they had sent it to another company who might be able to take it on. However, this second company did send a rejection slip and returned my chapters. 'OK', I thought, 'at least I tried,' and I put the papers away and forgot about them. Or nearly. Periodically my eyes would light upon the file on my computer marked 'Book' and I would open it up and read a little of the story. It had been a lot of work and it was quite interesting, and I thought how exciting it would be to see my name on the cover of a real printed book. Someone mentioned self publishing to me and I searched through Google to find a company that did this. I found one in London and I requested information from them and discovered that they would charge £2000 to produce my book. This was far too much money and once again, I put the whole question out of my mind and got on with the rest of my life. However, it wouldn't go away, and, periodically, I would think about it all again. I had £2000 and I discussed with Richard the idea of spending it on a book. He said that if I really wanted to do it, then I should go ahead. I went back to the computer and searched again for a self-publisher. This time I arrived at the website of an American company called iUniverse. They were much more accommodating than the company in London and offered several different publishing packages. They would create a single book for a very reasonable price, and from here the packages increased in service and price until the top priced package which included the services of an independent reader who would take the manuscript and provide a comprehensive report on its viability as a marketable product and give advice on improvements to be made. The package also included the production of the book and 35 copies. After that the author was to buy further copies at a reduced price for resale at the published price. It would also be available through internet sites such as Amazon and any bought in this way would bring me a royalty payment. The price was set by the length of the book. The only problem for me was that any royalties would be paid in dollars, but as I was not expecting to sell many books, I did not perceive this to be anything to worry about. The price of the top package at $695 (about £350) was so reasonable that I decided to go ahead and at the least we would have our record in a proper book form and I would have the experience of seeing our story in print.

I paid my money and was given a person who would oversee the whole process for me. We communicated via email and she guided me through. The first thing I had to do was to send the manuscript from my computer to hers and from there it was sent to the independent person for his report. The manuscript was in its very raw state, just as I had written it. I knew it would need going through carefully to correct punctuation and that some of the English needed attention. I waited for a fortnight until the report came back. When it did, I scanned through it, hardly knowing what to expect. Apart from the fact that it needed the punctuation correcting (line editing) there were only two criticisms. The title needed some kind of explanation and the book needed an introduction. All the sections dealing with content were extremely positive and I printed the report off and quickly ran to show Richard. He read through it and was as pleased as I was with it. The issue about the title was understandable. I had called the book 'The Ladies of Low Arvie' referring to the cattle, as all of the heifer calves we had named, including those which came unnamed from Bardennoch Hill with their mothers and needed to be registered as pedigree with the Galloway Society, were called Lady something of Low Arvie. The title of the book was ambiguous and could be thought to refer to other kinds of ladies. I discussed with my daughter what we could use as a subtitle and she suggested the saying 'Living the Dream'. This still lacked a specific reference to the content and so we made it 'Living the Farming Dream' which seemed to fit the bill. The question of the introduction was easily solved as I sat at the computer and wrote to my audience from my heart, explaining the thoughts that were behind our adventure and expressing the hope that any who read it might be inspired to follow their dream, whatever that might be. My helper at iUniverse was well satisfied with these two amendments and this just left the question of the line editing. IUniverse would arrange for this to be done but it came at extra cost, as someone outside the company had to be paid to do it and she told me this was costed at so much a word. The total charge would be something over $900, which would almost treble the cost of the book and so I said that I would do this myself. I spent three whole days going through the script, rearranging sentences and adding punctuation marks. Towards the end of the three days I became quite headachy with the work and, as our vet John Sproat pointed out when he had read the book, some of the commas ended up in the wrong place and there were a few too many here and there. However, by and large, the script ended up in a fairly reasonable and readable state. For an extra payment of $100, I could include photographs and we all felt that the book would benefit from the addition of these and so I sorted through my catalogue and found a few appropriate ones. These had to be sent through to the iUniverse website in America. We were still on dial up internet at this time and, as anybody who has used dial up knows, it is very slow and prone to crash. I stayed up late one night when the internet was least busy and began to download the pictures onto the iUniverse website. Some of them took a whole hour to go and three times the counter told me the progress had reached 97% before the whole thing crashed and I had to begin again. I never got to bed at all that night but at least the pictures had gone.

All that remained now was to produce a cover for the book and write the blurb that goes on the back. The cover was quite difficult, as most of the book was about the house we had bought and now it was altered by the addition of the extension beyond all recognition. I approached a professional photographer in Dumfries by the unlikely name (for Scotland) of Zvonco Kracun and he agreed to come and see me and discuss my needs. He told me that he had produced many book covers and I felt quite pleased that I had found him. Zvonco came out the day that Lady Elizabeth produced her first calf and the calf was named Zvonco in his honour. I explained to him the problem about the house and he asked if we had any photos of the old house on my computer. Together we searched through my picture file and came up with several that might be useful. We put these on a disk for him to take away and then he went off with his camera and took several more shots around the farm.

The result that he came up with is a stunning meld of eight different pictures and is more than adequate to describe in one image the contents of the book. I was thrilled with it and so was my iUniverse helper.

I then quickly completed the remaining portions of the book, including blurb for the back, contents page, dedications and epilogue and sent all these through. All that remained was to wait for the finished product.

The only slight disappointment I had when my nervous fingers had finally managed to open the package of thirty-five books, which arrived in late July 2005, was the appearance of the photographs which I had lost a whole night's sleep to download. They were only reproduced in black and white and some of my labelling did not look too professional, but by and large 'The Ladies of Low Arvie' is something I am quite proud of.

I visited most of the people named in the book and told them that it might be on sale in the town. Nobody raised any objections and so I took several copies down to Barry Smart's newsagent and book shop in Castle Douglas and he put them on display amongst the other books written by local authors. Soon he was ringing me for more, as the first consignment had sold out, and he has continued to stock them ever since. It sold well in the first months but sales then slowed as most interested people had either bought a copy or borrowed one. I began to receive letters from tourists who have bought the book and enjoyed it and several have even appeared at the door to meet us and tell us of their pleasure in reading it. It has not made the best seller list and has never been sold anywhere locally but in Barry Smart's shop but I am well satisfied with the reception it received. I have not made any profit from the book, in fact quite the reverse, but the experience was new and exciting and one which I may repeat if this current effort turns out to be as acceptable.

6

Tags

Since the BSE scandal of the 80s and 90s, it has been the EU ruling that all the calves that are born have to carry a tag in each ear, put there by the breeding farmer within 3 days of birth for dairy calves and 20 days for beef calves. Each farm has its own agricultural holding number, which in our case is 585065, and the farm is issued with the ear tags bearing this number along with the individual six digit number of the calf. The way we obtain these tags is not straightforward. There are several different manufacturers but we mere farmers are not allowed to communicate directly with them, but have to order the tags through an agricultural supplier, which, for us, is Tarff Valley Agricultural Supplies Limited. Tarff then place the order with the manufacturers, but, before the tags can be released to us, they must inform the Cattle Tracing System at the British Cattle Movement Service headquarters in Workington which numbers they are releasing. BCMS then enter these numbers onto our 'page' on their website. When Richard tags a calf, I then call up our page and enter in the details of that calf. The details are checked by the BCMS staff and then the calf is registered as being on our farm and its passport is sent to us. The passport shows the calf's details, its date of birth, breed, sex, dam and the date registered, and it contains several pages, each one printed with the same details in bar code form. There are also spaces at the front of the passport for our farm sticker to be affixed on the first page and

Richard signs and dates it and then the calf is 'legitimate'. If these processes are not carried out to the letter, the animal is not allowed to be traded or to enter the food chain or even to be reared for home consumption and is therefore useless. When the calf is sold to another holding, the sticker of the new owner is placed underneath ours and either one of the postcard pages is detached and sent to BCMS by both seller and purchaser or both parties register the movement on their relevant page on the BCMS website. When an animal is killed the passport has to be returned to BCMS and the fact of its death is recorded. Four times a year we receive from them a list of the animals that are registered on the system as being on our farm and we have to verify the details or correct them. In this way it is possible to know the whereabouts of every bovine animal in the country at any time. This is what is known as 'Traceability' and it is very strictly monitored. It is important as it means that all animals that come into contact with infection, such as Foot and Mouth disease, can be traced and tested quickly to help prevent spread.

Because we only have a small number of cows, I order the tags in batches of twenty-five. Yoghurt was Low Arvie calf number 49 and thus we only had one tag, number 50, left in the box. Accordingly on August 5th I telephoned to Tarff and ordered our next batch of twenty-five tags ready for the new calves that were due in September.

There are two types of tags that we are allowed to use. One is made up of two pieces of yellow plastic shaped like a small spade, with the 14 digit alpha-numeric number (they all begin with UK then the holding number followed by the individual number) impressed into the plastic and coloured black. One of the pieces has a sharp point protruding from it and the other has a hole for the point to fit into. Richard attaches these to the calf's ear in exactly the same way as human ears are pierced. The two parts of the tag are placed in the tagging pliers and then these are positioned over the calf's ear and closed, locking the tag into place through the ear. The process appears to cause the calf little in the way of discomfort and Richard prefers to do it as soon as he can after the calf is born. The second type of tag is made of metal and is all in one piece. It is shaped like an open triangle with the shorter, open side sharpened to a point. This tag is placed over the edge of the ear and nipped up tight with the pliers. If an animal loses one of the tags, which happens occasionally perhaps through constant rubbing against a gate, then a new tag has to be ordered with the same number and replaced in the empty ear as soon as possible after the loss. Dire consequences are threatened to any farmer found to have animals with less than the required two tags!

Richard prefers to use one of each kind of tag, as the metal ones are easier and quicker to insert in a calf that may jump up and run away or which may have a rather cross mother approaching fast, and he always puts this one in first. The yellow one is easier to read and is used to identify the animal around the farm. We are allowed twenty days to tag our calves, and once he has the first tag in, Richard feels he can relax a little if he is not able to get the other one in immediately, as at least the calf is numbered and there is sure to be opportunity to get the second tag in at some time before the twenty days are up. The mothers, even ours that are usually most gentle and placid, are very protective in the earliest days of a young calf's life and it can be a very dangerous process as he found with Gladeye. Once these early days are over and the mother has become a little less attentive, then the calf is usually running around and, obviously will not stand still, as it does not appreciate having its ear pierced. Unfortunately they do not understand the rules of the EU!

A few days after placing my order for the tags numbered 51 to 75 with Vicky at Tarff, the two new sets of tag, the plastic ones from Ritchey and the metal ones from a different manufacturer called Ketchum, arrived in the post and I put them away in the cupboard to await the arrival of the new batch of calves. The first one, number 50, arrived on September 1st when Silver Bell gave birth to a fine bull calf named Septimus. He was duly tagged and registered on the website and a few days later we received his passport which was stickered and signed and placed on a new pile in the passport cupboard. The next cow to calve was Jill on the 9th of September and she had a heifer, whom we called Lady Isla. She was number 51 and Richard was able to put in both tags, the first from the new batches, and I sat down at the computer to register the birth.

However, when I got on to the website and clicked on the drop down box containing the numbers that were allotted to us and where numbers 51 to 75 should have appeared, nothing happened. We are not allowed to put in the numbers ourselves, only to choose the correct one that appears on our listing. I tried again, but still nothing. Sighing deeply, I turned my swivel chair around to where the phone stood and picked up the receiver. I dialled the number of BCMS and waded through the options, pressing the required numbers until a human being asked if she could help. I explained my problem to her and heard her clicking away on her computer to bring up our record. 'You haven't been allocated those numbers,' she said. 'Oh, yes we have,' said I. 'No,' she said, 'those numbers do not appear on your page.' 'I know that,' I said, 'that is why I am calling you. Can you please enter them so that I can register the calf?' 'No, I can't do that,' she said, 'the tag manufacturers have to notify us that they are releasing tags with those numbers to you, and they haven't done that, so you can't have got the tags yet.' 'We have the tags,' I said, impatience rising in my soul, 'Number 51 is currently in the calf's ear, but I can't register her because the number isn't on our page.' Silence ensued at the other end of the phone. Eventually she said 'Well, can you ask the manufacturers to inform us that they have sent you the tags?' 'No,' I replied, 'I can't do that because I am not allowed to communicate with the manufacturers. We do not have their telephone numbers.' Silence again. 'Well, how do you order the tags from them?' she eventually asked. 'I telephone to my agricultural suppliers and ask them to order the tags for me.' 'Well, can you call them and ask them to phone the manufacturers and ask them why they haven't told us that they have released them?' It was becoming obvious that she was not going to solve the problem, so sighing deeply again, I agreed to do what she asked. I pressed my finger on the phone to cut the call off and dialled the number of Tarff. Vicky answered my call and I explained the problem to her. By now it was gone five o'clock and she said there would be no-one in the offices of either Ritchey or Ketchum, but she agreed to call them the next day.

When we went out the next morning, we saw that Beauty was missing from the herd, which was waiting in the shed for breakfast, and so Richard went searching for her and found her standing proudly in the corner of Brookfield while her new calf was enjoying his breakfast of milk from her udder. We called him Handsome and he was duly tagged with number 52.

Later that morning Vicky rang me to tell me that she had called both Ritchey and Ketchum. They had said that their records showed that they had followed the correct procedure and notified BCMS that they were releasing numbers 51 to 75 to us. I rang BCMS and, after going through the whole story again with a different BCMS person, I explained that both manufacturers were adamant that they had reported the release of the numbers. There was much clicking of computer keys and then the girl said, 'Well, can you ask them when they told us?' With mounting frustration, I wondered what farmers with hundreds of cattle and sheep on their farms would say, if this scenario happened to them and they had to waste precious minutes making so many calls. At least I had the time to do all this phoning, but it was very annoying even for me. I rang Vicky and put in a request to her to phone Ritchey and Ketchum again and get the date for me. She must have been as frustrated as I was, as the Tarff office is very busy, but she agreed to call them when she had time. A day or two later, I received the answer from her. The records of both Ritchey and Ketchum showed that they had each put the information through to BCMS on the same day, August 11th, and then posted off the tags to us. As soon as I got the call from Vicky, I rang BCMS and told the story a third time to yet a different person, this time including the date given by both manufacturers. 'Oh yes,' she said, 'that was the day our computers went down and we were unable to receive information.' I was so flabbergasted at the casual way she informed me of this, with thoughts of all the time wasted both by me and Vicky, not to mention the people at Ritchey and Ketchum and all the expense of so many phone calls that for a moment I was speechless. Looking back on the episode from the safe distance of the intervening months, I can still feel the anger that was growing in me and which exploded at her next words. Obviously totally oblivious to the trouble, time wasting and expense that had been caused, she went on airily, 'Can you ring them and ask them to put it through again, please? I can't put your numbers on the system until they do.' I could not trust myself to speak and I dropped the phone back into its cradle, little caring what the girl on the other end must have thought about my rudeness. I thought that I simply dare not ring Vicky again, and I went out to find Richard and tell him the latest development and vented some of my frustration in the telling. We wondered why, oh why they hadn't just asked for this to be done in the first place! Of course, I had to make the call because I needed to register our calves and it was clear that there was no way

I could do so without the numbers being entered on the page. With mounting trepidation, I went inside and picked up the phone again. Happily for me, Vicky was at lunch and so I was spared whatever her reaction might be, and I quickly left her a message with the request.

I don't know her personally, but she must be a nice lady, because she rang me later that day to say that she had rung Ritchey and Ketchum again and we grumbled together about the thoughtlessness and incompetence of BCMS in the matter. Altogether there had been fifteen telephone calls, most of them long distance, eleven of them being totally unnecessary and taking up time which could have been better spent by all involved.

However, by the time Honey gave birth to Horace on September 17th, the numbers had appeared in the drop down box and, thankfully, the new registrations were achieved with no further problem.

7

Heinz

It was by now the autumn of 2005. The next four calves arrived with little to cause anxiety and were soon gambolling around the fields full of health and happiness. This was our third year of farming, but, although we had been devastated by the suffering unwittingly caused to Yoghurt, now that he was returned to health, I still felt the same thrill of seeing the little animals exploring their environment. I spent as much time as I could with them in the fields, in between my other household chores and starting my new Open University course, which this year was level 2 Human Biology. The books for this had arrived in late September and, as well as the seven books I had to study, there were several tutorials to be attended at the Caledonian University in Glasgow. The Open University makes use of local University buildings for these tutorials when they are not needed for their own students and, consequently, they are held on Saturdays. To arrive on time for them, I needed to catch the 6.50a.m. train from Dumfries and did not arrive home until after 6p.m. in the evening, although the lessons were only three hours long. This obviously made for quite a tiring day, but I was enjoying the course and that made it easier to make the effort. To keep up the speed that I felt was necessary in following the required number of courses, I had decided to make the level 2 Reading Classical Latin my other course for the year. I knew this would not be as arduous for me as I have always enjoyed reading Latin and did

'A' level many years ago at school. I have periodically returned to the books I studied at school over the years, and so kept up some of my ability. This course was not due to begin until February and so I wanted to get the Biology course well under way, as all of that was new to me. I was also following two short courses, a level 1 Mathematics course to fill up my quota of 120 points at that level and a level 2 course about Fat (of which I have plenty!)

I mentioned briefly the excellence of the Open University system of education and, as further proof, I can cite my experience of the Spanish course in early 2005. To learn a foreign language effectively, there has to be an element of speaking and listening to a native speaker. To overcome the difficulties of this for students spread far and wide across the world, the OU provided audio cassettes, now replaced with CDs, which are used in conjunction with the books. There are also many tutorials to which the students go to meet the tutors, who are usually recruited from the country in question. This is fine for students in large cities, who are usually near enough to go to these tutorials, but for people who live, as I do, way out in the country, this is more difficult. In Scotland, these tutorials are only provided in Glasgow and Edinburgh and, as with the Biology lessons, it takes a whole day and more time is spent travelling than at the lesson. With the advance of technology, specifically the Internet, the OU has overcome this problem and now the language courses can be successfully completed in the comfort of one's own home. Students are provided with a computer programme which is a virtual block of lecture rooms, and once downloaded onto the computer and a pair of headphones with attached microphone purchased, it is easy to attend lessons. The programme allows listening and speaking, as well as having interactive white boards on which both tutor and students can write. My lessons were all held in the evening which suited our way of life admirably. There was a very committed set of students in my group and, as well as 'meeting up' for the lessons, we also logged on at weekends to practice what we had learned and we soon made a very strong friendship as well. We were situated all over the world. There was Norma in Australia, Janice in Mallorca, Jan in Tunbridge Wells, Neil in Ardnamurchan, in north-west Scotland and me in Dumfries and Galloway, and we spent two or three hours each week chatting away in our newly learned Spanish.

I became very friendly with Jan in Tunbridge Wells and we still keep in touch even though our studies are finished. She had decided to continue with the Spanish level 2 course, whilst I was diverting to Biology and Latin, but we enjoyed studying together so much, that I decided to buy the level 2 Spanish course books and study it along with her, although not, of course, sending in the assignments or sitting the exam. I thought I might do the course 'for real' the next year and this would be an excellent help. Richard and I spent two winters in Spain before we bought the farm and had made good friends there who spoke no English, so I was happy to improve my command of the language in any case. I soon found the course for sale on ebay (a lot of students sell their old course books and I bought many of them as it was a good way to see the course before enrolling and parting with the fairly hefty course fee charged by the OU). In this way I was effectively studying three long courses and two short ones in that academic year and Jan and I spent hours on the Internet reading and speaking together. So life was quite busy!

One day Richard and I convened a board meeting to look at the stock and plan for the next year (i.e. we sat at the kitchen table with the farm herd book). It would soon be time to get the bull again and we had to decide which cows were going to meet with him. We had to consider the winter rains that would turn our fields to mud, and cut down the number of animals if we could. We are charged with keeping the land in good condition on pain of death, or at least on pain of having the meagre subsidy that enables us to keep farming removed. It was necessary, therefore, to plan carefully which animals were worth keeping. The three Low Arvie heifers, Ladies Olga, Pete and Rebecca, were to have their first turn with the bull that autumn and so it seemed reasonable to part with three of the oldest cows who were at the end of their breeding life. Looking at the lists, we decided the first one to go should be old Gladeye. She had already missed getting in calf once and, in spite of living in close proximity to us whilst Yoghurt was recovering, she had never become in the slightest bit tame and remained a threat whenever she was approached. There was another old cow, Helena, who was of the same character and had once tried to attack Richard for no reason, so she went on the list. The third was to be Peggy, who was one of the oldest and was beginning to show signs of arthritis in her hips and back legs and we didn't think it would be fair to put her back to the bull again. These three would go when their current calves were weaned in the summer but in the meantime would not go back to the bull with the others. The last two had not yet had their calves and so we separated them from the rest of the herd and put them together in the small back paddock to await their time. We also decided to put Spot with them and give her a year off. She was now old but showed no sign of illness and so she would have her calf and a rest and then we would make the decision about her the next year. We left Gladeye and Yoghurt with the herd until the bull's arrival was imminent in the hope that Yoghurt would become more integrated.

It is always sad to part with animals especially when they have served us well, but we are running a business and cows cost a lot to feed and maintain, and so we just had to be sensible about it and not allow heart to rule head. We console ourselves that our cows have a good, long life and are well cared for throughout.

The first of the three cows in the paddock to calve was Peggy. Her calf was number 57 and so was called Heinz. Richard found him in the corner of the paddock early on the morning of October 29th. In spite of being old and experienced, Peggy was not the best mother in the world. Her first Low Arvie calf had been Wodan, who was born with wonky front feet and we had had a real struggle to raise him. She had tried to drag him all around the farm because she insisted on remaining with the other cows after his birth, instead of staying with her calf for a few days as the other cows did. We had managed in the end to get her to bond with him, but we were not impressed with her maternal instinct. For this reason I went out to check on the new calf frequently and the first few times, Heinz was sleeping in his corner and his mother was resting with the other two cows some way away. The next time I looked, he was standing looking forlorn and miserable giving intermittent cries, whilst she still sat with her sisters and did not appear to be taking any notice. I opened the gate and went to him. Straightaway, I could see that something was wrong. His eyes were open but there was no eyeball in the socket. Where his eyes should have been there was just a dark mass. With horror, I realised that he was blind! I hurried away to find Richard, and he agreed that the calf did not appear to have any eyes. He picked him up and carried him into the shed and we went back to get his mother. She grumbled and at first refused to move, but she was tamer than Gladeye and eventually we managed to manoeuvre her into the shed, where she showed no interest in the calf. We put her in the crush and Richard milked her so that I could at least feed him. We did not think he could have suckled since he was born, as he could not see. We let Peggy out of the crush and then shut them up together and were satisfied to see that Peggy now went to her calf and gave him a few licks. He looked a little less miserable and settled down in the dry straw to sleep. We went in the house and rang Roddy to ask for advice. He suggested that, since the calf was not ill, we might take him down to the surgery to be examined, thus saving the call out cost of a veterinary visit.

We decided to take him in the old van, rather than in the livestock trailer where he might try to get up and hurt himself through blundering about, and when the day's work was finished, I put on my oldest clothes, whilst Richard fetched old duvets and blankets to pad the floor and sides of the van. We then put Heinz in the back and I climbed in after him and attempted to hold him tight like a kind of human seat belt for the eleven mile journey to Castle Douglas. Richard and I were both upset, as we knew in our hearts that Heinz was blind and doubted very much that Roddy would be able to do anything for him. Furthermore, we could not see how he was going to survive and feared the outcome would be an injection of Nembutal. The journey was a nightmare, not made any easier by the twists and turns of the road and the fear of the little animal. He had only been born that morning into a bewildering black world and I could feel his heart pounding with fear through his ribcage as I held on to him as tightly as I could and tried to keep him calm with soft words. Although new born, he weighed around 45 kilos and with the jerking of the van, I found it very difficult to keep my balance and hold him firmly and, in spite of the blanket padding, my body was battered and bruised when we arrived at the vet's. Roddy came out immediately and confirmed that Heinz was blind and there was no hope of him ever being able to see. With trepidation, we asked him what the best thing to do was. To our surprise, Roddy did not even mention the option of putting him down. 'Oh, he'll be fine,' he said, 'Get him suckling and he will soon get used to the environment. This happens occasionally and most times they survive very well and learn how to cope.'

We put him back in the van and retraced our bumpy journey back home and let Heinz back to his mother. She seemed not to have missed him greatly, but did take an interest in his return. We watched for a while to see if he would suckle, but, although the instinct was obviously strong within him, he did not seek sustenance from the correct place and just sucked at his mother wherever he felt her. The cow's udder does not seem to be placed very conveniently, as the calf has to go searching diligently to find it and it is always a miracle to me that most calves get it right in a very short time. Lady Olga took just fifty-five minutes after her birth to find her mother's udder and it is always an immense relief when we see the calf suckling. The first milk that the mother produces is full of antibiotic properties that keep the calf safe from infection during the first months, until its own immune system is up and running, and it is vital that it gets this first milk, called colostrum, as soon as possible.

It was once more a question of milking the mother and feeding the calf from the bottle until he could manage to find her udder for himself and, with Heinz, this was going to be more difficult than usual! With just a faint sigh, Richard set about manoeuvring Peggy into the crush, while I fetched the jug and bottle from the kitchen, and we gave him his next meal. Once more it was going to be a time for patience and perseverance!

As we had expected, it was a very difficult job to get Heinz suckling. For several days we tried to point him in the right direction with no success, and each time we ended up milking Peggy and feeding him from the bottle. As with Yoghurt, he began to associate me with food, rather than his mother and we knew we had to sort things out urgently. Fortunately, Peggy was more compliant than Gladeye and did not try to attack us. She did seem to realise that we were trying to help and once more we resorted to the double cream treatment of her teats and each time Richard urged the calf towards her udder she stood still for him. This time it was the calf that was not cooperative and the more Richard urged him forward, the more he backed away. We smeared the cream onto his muzzle to get him used to the taste and tried to pull Peggy's cream covered teats towards him. He was still attempting to suckle but always went to her front legs and searched there before sucking at her hair.

We continued to try, and eventually, after five or six fruitless days, he did find the cream on her teats and we saw him give a few sucks. Goodness knows how many pots of cream it took, but once he had found the correct place, he was more amenable to Richard's guidance and every morning and evening for a while, Richard climbed over the trough into the shed and pushed Heinz to the correct end of his mother. Thankfully, after about three weeks, he got the idea and began to suckle successfully by himself.

We then had to decide on his future. Could he stay with his mother for the next two years until he was ready for slaughter? She was on the list for disposal but it was an option, although he would cost us much more to rear that way, as she would have to be fed too, and so there would be no profit in him at all and may even be a loss. Then one day, as I looked out of the kitchen window, I was struck with an idea. I could see the herd in the distance with the young calves running around and yet here by the gate stood Yoghurt all by himself. 'What if we put Yoghurt in with Heinz?' I asked Richard when he came in for lunch. 'He hasn't socialized at all with the others. He might be a good companion for Heinz.' It seemed to be an ideal solution, if it worked. Both mothers were due to go and if the calves did gel, they could stay together and both would be ready to leave the farm around the same time.

It did prove to be the way forward. We moved Yoghurt and Gladeye back into the shed with Heinz and Peggy and, when Heinz was suckling well and had grown up a bit, we put the four of them into the little field at the front of the farm. As Roddy had predicted, Heinz did get used to his environment and he and Yoghurt became companions for the remaining two years of their lives. Yoghurt became Heinz' eyes and he followed him happily around. When they were nine months old and no longer needed their mothers, Richard took them on their last journey and the two calves lived together in the old shed and the small paddocks for the next two years.

It was always sad to see Heinz, especially the few times he lost Yoghurt and he either stood forlornly calling to him, or turned round and round on the spot hoping to touch him, and I don't think I would raise another blind calf. However, we did our best for Heinz and I console myself that he had a reasonable life!

8

Insemination

We were not able to hire Zeppelin the bull any more because the three Low Arvie heifers were having their first encounter with reproduction and they were his daughters. We had kept in touch with Scott McKinnon at Moniaive who had bought our first batch of bullocks, seeing him at the market and at a few farm sales we attended. These two events serve the farmers as social occasions and most of the farming neighbours we know can be found at them. As well as conducting the business of the day, they are where we keep friendships alive. Farmers do not have much time for normal socializing, being occupied with keeping their animals fed and watered and all the other necessary jobs around the farm, such as maintaining equipment, making hay and silage or spraying weeds. The list is endless and these gatherings are important functions for us.

We also saw Scott's name often in the newspaper, as he was beginning to win many prizes with his growing herd of Galloways and so we rang him and asked if he might have a bull available for hire. We do not want to buy one of our own because we do not have the space available to keep him away from the cows and heifers when his services are not required. Some farmers run two groups of cows, ones which calve in the spring and the other calving in the autumn, and in this way the bull is occupied for most of the year, but we just use the bull for around three months from late November until the end of February, giving us a calving window of three months from September to December. The calves then grow up at roughly the same rate and can be grouped together for their next two years, until the bullocks go to make the nation's Sunday dinners and the heifers are ready to join the herd as breeding cows. The idea is that we have three groups for most of the year: cows with calves, yearling calves and two year olds. As the two year olds fulfil their purpose, the young calves are weaned from their mothers around the age of eight months to form the new yearling group and give the mothers two or three months to 'dry off' and prepare for their next calf and the old yearlings form the new group of two year olds. Our farm is not rich in good land as it is very low lying and the hillsides that don't belong to us on either side send their rainwater down to us to join that which falls directly on our land. For this reason in the early years we were not able to overwinter all the animals and had to lay our plans carefully to try and make our business as successful as possible. The system outlined above looks fine in theory but does not always work out so well in practice. Some animals do gain weight faster than others and it is not always possible to clear the two year old group as easily as we would like to. Also we (mainly me) have a habit of getting those cows which the bull does not get pregnant inseminated by artificial means, which gives us the odd calf or two outside the main age groups.

When Scott returned Richard's call, he told us that he did have a young bull that he would be happy to let us hire. His name was Klondyke Lord, a son of Blackcraig Gusto, and we were very happy to have projected calves with these two prestigious Black Galloway names on their pedigree certificates.

That year Richard decided to winter the breeding herd up at the far end of the farm in our Auchenvey field (named because it was the closest to Auchenvey Farm where our friends and neighbours Dot and Willie live.) The early winter months were not too wet, although the frosts began early, and so Richard left the silage fields open so that they could range around picking up the last blades of grass from them.

Auchenvey field is what is known as rough grazing and is not cut for silage, and so the herd are able to live in it through the winter when the grass is not growing and the ground becomes muddy. Once the rain comes, the silage fields are shut off to preserve the ground there from being churned up. All our cattle are fed most days of the year with cattle cake, a nutritious mixture of wheat, barley and sugar beet pellets mixed with vitamins and minerals to keep them healthy. Richard just varies the amount of this that they have according to other available food and the current status of the animals: he gives less to the dry cows and increases their portions when they have had their calf and are providing milk, and more for the animals that are in the fattening stages. Giving them a feed each day helps to keep them tame and enables us to gather them up when necessary by rattling a bucket of food at them! Richard feeds them each morning and this is also the time when he checks them for lameness or other health problems and sometimes combs their tangled coats, which they love.

The last calf of the batch was born in early November and when he was up and running we let the herd go through the gates towards Auchenvey with Lord and closed off the gate at the far end Inbye field nearest to the farmhouse. They roamed around the silage fields and eventually made their leisurely way to the far end of the farm.

One day before the winter really set in and Richard had closed the gate at Auchenvey, I went for a walk through Inbye and intended to continue on through Brookfield, across the ford and up into Low Knowe. This is a favourite walk of mine and I do it often in fine weather to watch the seasons change and just enjoy the peace and tranquillity of the farm. As I set off that day, I could see the herd over to the south west grazing lazily amongst the rushes in Auchenvey. I opened the gate into Brookfield and, as I passed through, I found Lady Olga lying just behind the wall. As she saw me, she got up and began to walk towards me. I saw immediately that all was not well. She was very lame in one of her back legs and I held the gate open for her to hobble through and then shut it behind us and we walked back slowly together up to the farm. I called to Richard and we got Olga into the old shed, which Gladeye and Peggy and their calves had not long vacated, being now in their winter quarters in the small paddock at the front. It seemed that that year we were always destined to have someone in the old shed, which had become in the nature of our sick bay. I always enjoyed having animals in there, even though it meant something was amiss with them, because it was near to the house and I could go out often to see them and tend them.

We were very touched that Olga had made her way back home when she had had her problem and, by the way she came with me and entered the shed, it was clear that she knew where to find the help she needed. She was very lame and we never knew what caused the problem, but it may have been during her first encounter with Lord that something had happened, either he had slipped off her, or she had been taken by surprise and twisted awkwardly. Whatever it was, the injury was quite serious and she stayed for several weeks in the shed and rested, until she had fully healed. She didn't go back to the herd until almost the end of Lord's sojourn with us and when Roddy came in the spring to scan the cows for pregnancy, she was one of the three that were empty.

Of the other two, one was an old cow also called Peggy (many farmers call their cows by the same name) and we decided to part with her, and the other was Gina who was not old, but was one of the original calves that had come with the cows from Bardennoch Hill. We decided that it was time for Peggy to leave us but I suggested (tentatively!) to Richard that we might have Olga and Gina inseminated, possibly with semen from a Belted Galloway bull. When we first bought the farm we had decided to buy Belted Galloway cows as they were a little idiosyncratic and are a powerful symbol of the Galloway region, but the recent Foot and Mouth epidemic had taken out many herds and we could not find any Belties to buy. We had been fortunate to buy the Ladies of Low Arvie as a complete herd from a farm in the area that was selling up, but they were Black Galloways. The two breeds are related and the animals have the same conformation, so they can interbreed successfully and I had been told that the gene for the white belt was dominant and we stood a chance of getting calves with one even from a Black Galloway mother.

As usual, Richard was amenable to my suggestion and we began to look into the process. There are two ways to engineer the insemination process. One is to wait until the cow comes into season naturally, but this entails watching them closely until they are being ridden by the other cows, or even riding the other cows themselves. There is usually a slight discharge of mucus from the vulva at this time, which serves as a second indicator. It would be very fortunate indeed if both our candidates came on heat at the same time, allowing us to inseminate them together and to have them calve at approximately the same time, so to follow this route would more than likely mean different calving dates. The second way is to manufacture the season by the use of hormone implants, and this would bring them on heat at the same time. Many dairy farms use this method as they usually only use artificial insemination for the creation of their calves, making their planning easier. We decided to go for the natural route. Cows come into season approximately every twenty days if the egg is not fertilised and so we decided to keep Olga and Gina close by so that we could monitor them closely. The pregnant cows were put in Eastside field with their, by now, growing calves, and the yearlings were banished up to Auchenvey to grow on up there. The changeover was because we were still in the Rural Stewardship Scheme, which we joined in 2003, and which dictated the dates we were allowed to mow the grass and graze the cattle in the silage fields after the mowing. We would need to wean the calves as soon as the grazing was permitted and keeping them closer to the farm in Eastside meant that this would be easier to achieve when the time came. The calves would stay in Eastside and the cows would be moved onto the silage land for the last month or two of their pregnancy and to calve.

Olga was the first to come into season and on March 6th I phoned the AI company, Genus, and requested a visit. The only Belted Galloway semen they had available was from a bull called Mochrum Kingfisher, so we didn't have to pick and choose, but Dame Flora MacDonald who raised the Mochrum herd was a very well known name in the farming world. In fact we had met and talked with her once, just before coming to Low Arvie when we were choosing our breed, and we had no qualms about using semen from her bull. Richard had got Olga once more into the old shed and it didn't take long to put her in the crush when Jenny, the AI lady arrived. Nor did it take long for the deed to be done! Jenny dressed herself in her long plastic gown and took a long, thin stainless steel syringe and the plastic straw containing the semen from the stock in the boot of her car. Before I could even get to the shed to watch, she and Richard were back in the yard talking whilst Jenny took off her gown and then she got into her van and drove away. Apparently, all had gone well. Jenny had told Richard that Olga was in the correct mode, with her cervix opened to allow the passage of semen through and that come nine months and ten days we should have our first Belted Galloway calf. Of course, it wouldn't be a full Beltie, just a Beltie cross, but it was quite exciting, nevertheless. Gina followed the same route some nine days later and when she was inseminated, again by Jenny with Mochrum Kingfisher semen, we put them into Eastside with the rest of the herd to await their calves.

9

Walls

My only concern when contemplating the move to Scotland from South Yorkshire in 2002 had been the situation of my Mother. She was by then 90 years old and, since my father had died in 1997, I had been her main support and help. I did not feel happy about leaving her alone in Yorkshire, but she had lived in the same house for sixty-three years and I was not sure about the effect of leaving this environment would have on her. However, I was also very worried about what would become of her if she remained there without me to solve her problems and keep an eye on things. The problem, however, was easily solved, thanks to her indomitable spirit and the lucky discovery of the Abbeyfield Society. She had had no hesitation in uprooting herself and moving into the sheltered care of the Society's home, Bothwell House, in our nearest town, Castle Douglas. She settled there very quickly and passed the next three years very happily. I visited two or three times each week and life for her was very easy and she enjoyed the relative freedom to pursue her own interests, whilst being well looked after and still having me to oversee things for her. As time went on, though, I watched her slow deterioration into dementia and, although she remained very much the Mother I had always known, this deterioration showed itself in many small ways. Gradually she lost the ability to complete the Telegraph cryptic crossword which had been her first task of the day for as long as I could remember and before. One of the saddest times on this stage of her journey was the realisation that reading was no longer the pleasure that it had always been for her. I had fostered a very good relationship with Martin, who keeps the Douglas Books shop just up the road from Bothwell House and each week I would purchase three or four second hand books from him and then re-sell them the next week and collect some more. One day she asked me not to bring any more as she found that she could not remember what she had read the previous day and the books were no longer the joy they had been. She had also stopped going out for her daily walk and no longer wanted to go to the church hall next door for the Mother's Union meetings. I tried different ways to help her remember things, buying notice boards and calendars to fill in the various activities and putting her daily dose of tablets into boxes with marked compartments, but it became apparent to me over the latter half of 2005 that her loss of short term memory was a real problem. She could no longer remember when meal times were and what time, or even if, her carers would come to help her dress and undress.

One day the housekeeper met me on one of my visits to Bothwell House and told me that Mother was becoming distressed at this loss of memory and had begun to wander around the house during the night wondering what she should be doing. It was clear that something had to be done. On Christmas Eve 2005 she moved to the care of the local residential home at Carlingwark House, once again settling in easily and for several months she regained some of the lost confidence, as she was no longer responsible for remembering anything, because there was always someone there to fetch her for meals and see to her needs. I continued to visit regularly and was content that she was happy again.

It was on returning home from visiting Mother one day that I found a message on the telephone from our neighbour, Dot at Auchenvey farm, telling us that a car had crashed through the wall at the far end of the farm into the field where the cows were grazing. Richard was also out in town that morning and, as I wasn't sure how long he would be, I got back in the car and drove up to the field where I saw a red Peugeot car through the wall at right angles to the road. It had crossed the verge and punctured the wall, finally coming to rest at the edge of the field. There was nobody either in the car or around the area and I wondered where the driver was. However, with the car where it was, the hole in the wall was effectively blocked and the cows were over at the far side of the field and not showing any interest in the event. Feeling that they were safe for the moment and expecting Richard to return in the very near future, I returned home. However, when I got back, I thought that I should have taken the registration number of the car. I looked out of the window, hoping to see Richard in the van coming along the road. After a few minutes without any sign of him, I decided that I had better return to the car and take the details. There was still no one around and I wrote the car's registration number down and once more returned home. A further quarter of an hour passed before Richard came back and I was able to tell him about the car. He went to look at it and survey the damage caused, hoping to find the driver and sort out the problem. But, when he had covered the half mile, all he found was the hole in the wall, no car and no sign of anyone. Happily the cows were still at the far side of the field and Richard was able to take up one of the unhung gates we had at the farm to make a temporary fence across the hole. How fortunate for me that I had gone back and taken down the details of the car!

With no information and no contact from the driver, we had no alternative but to ring the local police, who instituted a search of their records using the registration number I was able to give them. Very soon, they rang us to give us the name of the driver and to tell us they had contacted her and discovered that she had been trying to retune her car radio and had lost control of the car. She had been on her way to work in Dalry, some twelve miles from the farm and, having got out of the car uninjured, she had walked away from the scene of the crash and used her mobile phone to contact the local garage in Dalry to ask them to come and recover her car. They had obviously done this very quickly in the time between my last trip to get the car details and Richard's return home. It was clear that she was hoping that she had contrived to get her car removed without letting us know about the damage to the wall and, hopefully, without having to repair it. She probably knew that dry stone walls (dry stane dykes as they are called in Galloway) are very expensive to build as each stone must be put in its place by hand and the wall must first be demolished for several feet either side of the repair to key the stones in properly. The police told her that she must come and see us and set about putting things right. It was very difficult for her to do this, but having no choice, she came that night on her way home and we were able to claim on her insurance to get the wall repaired. We felt she had got off lightly, not so much because she had tried to get away without repairing the wall but because she had removed her car and left our cattle at liberty to wander on to the road causing a hazard both to themselves and other motorists. Just thank goodness the event was concluded with harm only to the wall and her pride and not to person or animal!

We have a mile of road frontage at Low Arvie, and the drive entrance is half way along this mile on a fairly dangerous bend. The stretch of road which leads from this bend eastwards towards the village is between our Eastside field on one side and a fairly steep hill on the land of Arvie Farm on the other. In the winter the sun is too low to shine on the road over this hill and so the road becomes quite treacherous in frosty weather because it remains icy for the whole time that the temperature stays low. For some reason best known to themselves, the Council workmen resurfaced this stretch of road in the autumn of 2005 with smooth tarmac and it was clear to us that the winter weather would cause severe problems for motorists. This was proved to be the case, when, during the first cold spell, a lady's car slid off the road and grazed the Eastside wall for a distance of some fifty yards, before finally coming to a stop. The irony was that she had driven all the way from East Anglia in bad weather conditions and was within ten miles of her home when her accident happened. The car had not knocked the wall down, but it had moved it from its foundation making it unsafe, and some seventy yards of it had to be taken down and rebuilt. This lady informed us immediately and we were able to make the repair with no trouble.

The next episode was less serious to our walls but provided a welcome diversion to our winter routine. We were getting up early one dark Sunday morning, when I looked out of the window and could see flashing orange lights by the end of the drive. We continued to get up and went downstairs and from the windows there, we could see the wavering light from a torch by the closed drive gate and, in its light, a pair of human legs on the other side of the gate. Richard went out and found a man standing there. He had not come through the gate but had stood there illuminating his person, hoping that we would see him, in order that we were not scared by the approach of a stranger knocking on the door at such an early hour on a dark winter's morning. I found this to be very thoughtful, as the man had no idea who lived in the house and did not want to frighten the occupants who might be old and frail. We invited the man into the kitchen and he told us his story. He was the director of an asbestos removal company in Clacton-on-sea and he was transporting two of his workers from one job in Troon to another job in the South, which was to begin the next day. We asked why he was travelling along our narrow and windy road instead of along the faster and, in winter conditions, safer A75. It seemed that he had put his destination into his Satnav and asked it for the shortest route. Since our A712 does cut off a portion of the A75, this was why he had encountered the 'ice rink' at the end of our drive and his Renault Espace had ended up in the ditch alongside the wall. Happily he was a member of the AA and, whilst he rang for their assistance, Richard went down to the road to inspect the damage as best he could in the darkness and to invite the other two occupants of the car into the house. None of them had received any injuries and while we waited for the AA, we sat around the kitchen table and partook of toast and tea and chatted. Neither the men nor Richard had seen any serious damage to the body of the car but it was tilted down with its near side in the ditch, and Richard wanted the AA man to inspect the car before offering to pull it out with the tractor. There are stones buried just beneath the surface of our land and the man could have been unlucky enough to hit one of these, causing unseen damage to the chassis of the car.

The director was very impressed, when just three quarters of an hour later, we saw the approach of the AA van in the early light that had started to show in the sky whilst we breakfasted. He told us that he had expected to wait much longer out in the country, and that the last time he had had to call the AA out on an English motorway, he had waited more than three hours for them to arrive. This is one of the myths about life in the country. We find that all the services, being less stretched by the fewer numbers of people, are far quicker to respond to calls for help than in the more built up areas of the south.

Now that the light was increasing by the minute, the men went down the drive once more to inspect the car more fully. They all agreed that the damage did not appear to be very great and the AA man thought that the tractor pulling idea was the way to go and so Richard obliged. Soon the car was brought up into the yard where the damage could be finally assessed. There was no leakage of water or fuel and all appeared to be intact with the underside of the car. There were a couple of dents in the side and it was streaked with mud and grass stains but that was all. It hadn't contacted the wall at all. They agreed that the car should be fully driveable and the AA man left to go to his next call. The company director put his hand in his pocket and brought out a large wad of twenty pound notes. Peeling three of them off he gave them to Richard, telling him to take me out to lunch and, not listening to our complaints that the amount was far too much for the little help we had given, he and his men got into the car and drove away. We went back inside the house and Richard placed the notes on the kitchen table. We looked at them in astonishment, and then, laughing to each other, realised that this was the most, or in fact the only money, that Richard had 'earned' since we had come to the farm some four years earlier and we decided that it would be far more lucrative than farming if we could rely on this kind of episode happening on a regular basis!

The third occurrence on that icy road was more serious. We were having breakfast one morning soon after, when we heard a big bang, and on running to the window we could see the wheels of an upturned car still spinning in the road. Richard ran down to see what had occurred, and found that the lady in the car behind had stopped and was helping the lady driver of the upturned car to climb out. She had already rung for the emergency services and the driver, who was injured but able to walk, had just been brought into our kitchen when the paramedics came bumping up the drive in their ambulance. In a very short time we could also see that the police and a fire engine had arrived at the car. We were not called upon to do more than share our kitchen with those involved and the lady was soon taken off to the hospital, whilst the police and firemen dealt with the car. We did, however, talk to the police about the stupidity of resurfacing this particular road in such a dangerous way, and they called the Council and asked them to replace the tarmac with something more suitable. As soon as the winter weather abated and the spring arrived, they came and spread chippings, which do give a better grip. As expected, there have been far fewer accidents since then, but it still pays to be careful when the winter comes. It has also prevented any more lucrative work for Richard and his tractor!

10

Plans

It had always been Richard's wish to keep our male calves from birth right through to the time they are ready for slaughter. Galloways take at least two years to reach maturity and probably even longer. This is the way to make the most money in beef rearing, but the state of the land, its wetness and bogginess when we first came to Low Arvie meant that, except for Heinz and Yoghurt, whom we knew we could never sell to anyone else owing to Heinz' blindness, there was not enough room to keep them all over two winters. Hence the fact that we had been lucky enough to sell our first two batches to Scott as they approached their first birthday. We worked hard on draining the land and recovering as much as we could from the rushes. There were plenty of acres to support all the animals we needed to, but previous years of neglect after the death of Davy McQuaker in 1996 had allowed the rushes to take over many of the acres and, although grass did grow between them, it was impeded by the yearly increase of rainfall that was held between the roots of the rushes and favoured these tenacious plants rather than allowing the grass to grow plentifully. This rush covered land needs to be mowed and Richard is not able to do this as often as is necessary because of the climate we have to endure. The tractor can only get on to this land in the very driest times and over the early years of our occupation this was very infrequently. He had also needed to buy the correct machine, which, at a cost of four thousand pounds, had had to wait until we made some money to buy it. This machine arrived in the summer of 2005 and so clearance of the rushes was able to begin as soon as the land dried out in August of that year. The machine is a flail topper, a bit like a large lawn mower with great blades on a rotating cylinder. It cuts the rushes and chops the stalks into very small pieces which then shrivel and dry up, allowing the sun to assist the grass to flourish. The weather was dry enough that year to allow Richard to mow most of the rushes around the silage fields, where the good grass that we cut for winter feed grows on the higher knolls and the rushes spread around the knolls on the lower parts. If we could recover the grass from the rushes it would double the grazing ability of these fields, once the good grass was cut and the silage harvested in July. When the rushes were mowed, these parts of the fields began to take on an air more like the grassy parts and the cattle mooched round and round grazing the wet parts as well as the dry ones. We knew that this mowing would have to be repeated at least each year to keep the rushes at bay, as the winter rain would allow them to grow again and they would take back the land if they were not kept in check.

In the summer of 2005, we had received news that might help us to achieve Richard's aim of keeping the bullocks for their full lifetime more quickly than we had expected. The Scottish Executive or the EU or whoever makes the rules which govern Scottish farming, opened up a new grant scheme which was to run for a very short time to the end of the year. They would give a grant of up to 50% of the cost of new agricultural buildings. Richard began to think that we might profit from this grant and purchase a new, large shed in which we could keep the bullocks in the very wettest times, thus preserving the land from their feet. It was essential to do this because the subsidy scheme which had come into operation in Europe at the beginning if 2005 decreed that any farmer who didn't keep his land in Good Agricultural and Environmental Condition (or Gaec pronounced Geek, which we thought admirably fitted the people who make the rules we have to follow) was liable to have their subsidy withheld. There are a lot of people who disagree with these subsidies, but believe me, they are what keeps British farming afloat and without them the cost of food in our supermarkets would have to double or treble in order to maintain the farming fraternity. If the subsidies didn't exist and people were not prepared to up their food bills by such a large amount, many farmers would just have to give up farming altogether. Furthermore, it is our animals grazing and the production of their winter food which keeps the British countryside looking as it does and so the subsidies are a very essential part of the economy.

We began to look at what we needed to do to get the grant for our new shed and soon discovered a whole raft of conditions that needed to be met. First of all, we had to produce a business plan, proving that the shed could help us increase our output and this had to be drawn up by a professional person. In essence our plan was simple: we had some cows, they had calves each year which we couldn't raise to maturity because of the nature of our land, the new shed would enable us to finish our calves on the farm and even allow us to buy more from other farmers as Scott had bought ours, thereby upping our production by somewhere near 100%. Of course, it wasn't good enough for us to tell this plan to the Executive, but in order to help us produce a 'proper' official business plan, they would allow us a grant of 50% of the cost of the plan up to £800. They also provided us with a list of persons who would draw up a plan acceptable to them. I rang the first three on the list, explaining the simplicity of our operation and plan and asked what their charge would be. I was disappointed but not very surprised when each of them came back with the same figure: £800. It appeared that they were setting their charge according to the maximum figure allowed by the available grant, regardless of the complexity or simplicity of the plan required. I was not happy with this and felt that they were just taking the maximum amount of money out of the public purse. I rang someone we knew who works in the Agricultural department of the Executive and told him of my concern that this would be a waste of money and asked for his advice. He was able to give me another name, a man, he said, who might be more amenable to complete our plan for the true value of it, but which would also be acceptable to the department. I rang this man and he agreed with my assessment of the situation and said that he would come and see us to discuss our small operation and see what he thought a more reasonable cost would be.

After two or three meetings he drew up our business plan and sent us a bill for £400, thus saving both us and the public purse £200 each. Together with this business plan, I had to make costings and get quotations for all the work required to erect the shed. This included site preparation, gates, fences, the provision of electricity and water and the drainage work for which we had to get clearance from SEPA, the Scottish Environmental Protection Agency, who needed to be satisfied that no effluent from the shed would be allowed to pollute the water course on the farm, as well as the shed itself. We were also proposing to include a new cattle handling system in a part of the shed and this needed to be costed too. When I had all the quotations and the clearance letter from SEPA, I placed these with the application form and the business plan in a large envelope and posted it all off to Dumfries.

It all had to go before a committee who would look at the plans from all the farmers who wanted to take advantage of the new scheme. We might get the full 50% or we might get nothing depending on the number of applications and the viability of the other plans.

When the reply came, it was neither good news nor bad news, but gave us further headaches of decision making, for they had offered us, not 50% and not nothing, but just 25% of the cost of the shed.

We got this response from the Executive at the beginning of 2006 and, being given just 25% was perhaps the worst answer we could have got. It meant that Richard would have to invest a much larger chunk of capital into the project, but, on the other hand, the 25% was a lot better than nothing. To have failed altogether in the application would have meant that there was no decision to be made as we could not have gone ahead. On the other hand, to have been granted 50% of the cost would have also meant no decision to be made, as the benefits the new shed would give to the farm would far outweigh our input of the additional 50%, and we would have been very happy to go ahead straight away. I could not help Richard in making the decision, as it was his capital that would have to be spent and I left it to him to think around the problem for some weeks. There was a time limit to the offer and we had to send a form back, giving our decision within six months and so, when Richard had not come up with a decision one way or the other by March, I suggested that it was time to jump one way or the other fairly soon. Richard always takes a long time to think about things, whereas I am very impulsive and would have decided one way or the other as soon as the offer was received.

I think my decision would have been not to go ahead, but just carry on as we were and I quite expected that Richard would come to same conclusion. There was another consideration, too, as putting up the new shed with a financial input from the government meant that they would monitor the effect of it on our finances for five years, effectively committing us to remain at Low Arvie following the same regime of farming for that time. However, Richard was prepared to make this commitment and he could foresee better than me the great benefit that the new shed would be, both to our farming operation and as an increase to the value of the farm when, or if, we eventually come to sell. In early April, he told me that he thought we should go ahead and accept the money and so on the 19th of that month we went to Robinsons of Dumfries and placed an order for the shed. It was to be 100 feet long by 40 feet wide.

We had spent a long time with paper and pen drawing up our ideas for dividing the space in the shed in the most useful configuration and the final result would give us a wide passage way in the middle bounded by feed barriers down one side closing off a large area 40 feet square at one side which, with access to a small paddock on one side and to the lower half of our Inbye field on the other, would give enough space to house about twenty animals. The other side of the passage way would be divided into two, giving a smaller bedding area which had access to the other half of Inbye to house more cattle, and the new handling area, with an upmarket crush where the animals could be attended to in a much safer and more convenient way than at present, in the other half. There was also room to create two smaller pens in this area where single animals could be isolated should the need arise. It was a large undertaking but, undoubtedly, it was a very attractive proposition.

The decision was further complicated by the need to inform the Council of the plan. We did not need planning permission as such, but we did need to get a form from them stating that we didn't need planning permission, which seemed a bit crazy to me. The cost of this form was £50! This was all achieved fairly painlessly and in due course the letter arrived saying that we did not need planning permission. We did, however, need to comply with building regulations and for this we had to give all the details of the project and, hopefully, receive the Building Warrant that would allow us to go ahead. The price of this Building Warrant was based on a sliding scale dependent on the cost of the shed. When Richard finally decided to proceed, he filled in the Council forms and took them down to the planning office in Castle Douglas with a cheque for the required amount indicated in the paperwork for a building costing £14000, which was the price of the shed. Their response was annoying. They rang him to say that he hadn't paid enough money, and when he enquired why, he was told that he had to include the full cost of the whole project in the calculation including gates, feed barriers, electrical work and drainage and this they estimated would be £53000. Unless he paid the extra money for a building of this price, he would not get the Warrant. Their calculation was far in excess of the true cost and we spent further hours working this out, eventually coming to the result of £23000. This cut down the cost of the application by some £400 and so was an exercise well worth doing.

However, the Council had not finished with us yet. They next informed us that they required a structural engineer's report regarding the shed itself, listing all the components used to build the shed and fix them together to be sure that it was a safe structure. Richard told them that we were not building our own shed, but were purchasing an 'off the shelf' model from an agricultural supplier who would also be erecting it, and that there were many of the same model to be found on farms all around the district. It made no difference, they still required the report and so of the £400 saved on the application cost, £270 had to go on an engineer's report, which we obtained from the suppliers. The Council finally gave up asking us for money and we got the Warrant giving us the go ahead in late April.

When we placed the order with Robinsons, they said that they had a few orders to fulfil and that we would have to wait two or three months. I said that this was no problem and that as long as they built the shed before the rains of the winter came, all would be well. They promised to have the work done by August at the very latest!

We immediately set about preparing the site. There is no flat land at all on Low Arvie, and the only area where the shed could go was in Inbye field where about half of the area to be covered had only a gentle slope and then the remainder began to fall away very steeply. This had to be all made up level and after scraping the earth off the top to give a fairly solid base, Graham

McQuaker delivered load upon load of rock from their quarry to level the site. This work was all finished by the end of May and we sat back to await Robinsons and the shed.

When we had heard nothing by the end of July, we rang to see how the order was progressing. The shed would soon be with us, we were told. On September 13th they said that they were just manufacturing the shed and it would be with us in 'a couple of weeks'. The autumn rain began to fall heavily that year in the second week of October. The shed components were delivered on the 21st of October. The erectors came on the 25th October. They spent the wettest week of the year erecting the shed!

The vertical girders along the back of the shed had had to be made different lengths to cater for the lie of the land, so that they could all be seated on solid foundations. The day they were putting these in, we had to go out. When we arrived home, the builders had gone, but we could see they had not been idle and six upright steel girders stood proudly setting in their concrete bases in a nice straight line along the back edge of the shed. The only problem was that they had been inserted in the wrong order and the tops of the six girders were describing a wonderfully wavy pattern across the darkening sky!

Several of them had to be removed the next day and replaced in the correct order to create the straight line required to fix the roof.

All the while they were working, the rain poured down, as only it can in Galloway, and by the time the shell of the shed was finished and the roof was protecting the ground underneath from the rain, this ground, which Richard had lovingly levelled and packed down in May, was churned up by their machines into a beautiful hippopotamus wallow! We had no choice but to leave the whole area to dry out and so the project was put on hold and nothing further was done until the next spring.

I I

Sales and Expenses

2006 proved to be a very busy year for us folks at Low Arvie. The calves that were born in the previous autumn were all doing well. Heinz and Yoghurt had settled down to their life together and the arrangement was proving to be working well.

Late in 2005, we had held another board meeting and decided that once again we had too many animals for the winter and we needed to downsize the herd once again before the worst of the weather came. We took the very hard decision to part with some of the Bardennoch Hill heifers who had borne their first calf during the summer, just before Yoghurt was born. Of the nine heifers that had calved, six had had heifer calves and we decided to sell four of these with their calves at foot. Richard rang the two markets in the area and said that we wanted to sell these animals off the farm and not through the market ring and to let us know if anyone approached them to buy Galloways. Harry Begg at Dumfries market was the first to ring us. He had found a man who was in a similar situation to us. He had retired from his mainstream job and had bought a house and land in the Scottish borders and was looking for a few Galloway cattle to put on his land. Harry arranged to bring him over to see the cattle and so, very reluctantly I allowed Richard to separate four of the heifers with their calves for Harry and Tommy to see. It was much more difficult for us to let these animals go than the previous sale we had made

61

when Scott and John had bought the first year's calves, because these heifers had come to Low Arvie as small calves with their mothers and had spent their first months with us in the big cattle shed. We had fed them several times each day and had seen them grow from small calves into fine Galloway cows. Because of our constant contact with them that first winter, we had come to know them individually and had become very attached to them. But it was out of necessity that we had come to sell them and I just hoped that Tommy would be as good to them as we had been. They had been in with Klondyke Lord and the other cows for several weeks before he came to pick them up on the 8th December 2005 and as well as the four cows and four calves, he was probably getting four more unborn ones too. He did seem to be a nice man and was thrilled with the cows and we promised that one day we would go and visit him at his farm near Kelso.

In late January of 2006, the weather turned really bad and the ground began to look very muddy and churned up, so we had to decide once more to lessen the load and sell some more of our stock.

When we had gone to talk to Scott about hiring one of his bulls, we also had talked about him buying our second batch of steers to service the garden centres. His stock of Galloways was growing, but had not yet become big enough to provide all the meat that was required and so he said he would be happy to buy our second crop of calves born in the autumn of 2004 when they were ready. We rang him and he agreed to come and see them and talk about the price he would pay. He came to 'interview' them and said he would take them. He offered his usual fair price and we were very pleased to be able to sell them off the farm. As we sat chatting over a cup of tea, when the deal was done, he told us that he had bought some land of his own in Moniaive and was hoping to set up his own operation and run it for a few years along with that of his boss. When he came to retire as farm manager, he would carry on this smaller farm on his own account. He had already purchased the land and was looking for a few Galloway heifers to stock it with. He said that he would be very happy to purchase any of our heifers that we wanted to sell. I fetched the herd book and checked through the list of heifers that were old enough to leave the farm. This would reduce our numbers even further for the winter and would mean that we could be assured that they would be well cared for and would be near enough for us to visit. Scott was also very keen to show his animals and, if he won prizes with any of those with Low Arvie in their pedigree, it would be good advertising for us. We had the two remaining heifers from the summer calving that Tommy hadn't bought and six from the second Low Arvie calving of the Bardennoch Hill cows. We contemplated his offer and, in the end decided to let them all go to Scott. We had enough cows to calve the next autumn, when we hoped our land would be improved enough for us to keep more of the calves to replace any old cows that had come to the end of their breeding life the next year. It was a deal that suited us all and they left us on the 1st of February 2006.

We pass through Moniaive quite frequently and several times a year we drive up to Scott's land and we have watched the heifers grow into fine cows and go on to produce calves for him each year.

Selling so many of our animals left us in a good position for the winter, and also helped with our accounts, which were still looking very sick. We were still spending a lot of money on equipment for the farm and a few bad investments in second hand equipment which didn't last long had taught us that we needed to buy better machinery which cost a lot of money. We were still improving the tracks, using load after load of quarried stone and Richard had come up with a plan to create new roads which would make it much more convenient to move stock around. The layout of the fields with the house and building in the middle meant that you had to go through many of the fields to get to the far end. This made it difficult to keep the different groups of cattle separate at all times, but with the simple addition of better tracks and a new road along the edge of one field, there would be several routes from the buildings to all the fields. The boggy peat that covered much of the land made this process difficult and expensive. The peat surface had to be scraped off and then Richard begged half ton polypropylene fertiliser sacks from all our neighbours and these were laid on top of the scraped peat in a thick layer. Large stones were laid on top of these and then a smooth surface made with smaller crushed rock. It was all packed down and rolled with the tracks of a digger.

The other problem with not having good tracks around all the fields meant that constant tractor work, especially at silage time when each bale has to be collected and transported individually, takes a heavy toll on the grass and leaves tractor tyre marks scarring the land for months until the grass manages to cover them. We still have not remade all the tracks, but the new road has made a big difference to keeping the land in better condition as well as giving a much more flexible system of cattle movement between the fields.

I feel that we can be very proud of what we have achieved with the 120 acres of wet and boggy land that we came to in 2002. There is still a way to go to fulfil all the plans we have, and we know that we will never win the battle against the myriad rushes that cover most of the acres. It is a constant fight against their tenacious roots which are permanently fed by the high water table beneath the peat, but for one middle aged man, who just has the support of a weak and feeble woman, the improvement that is evident in most areas of the farm is an achievement that none can doubt.

12

Mother

Selling so many of our animals over the early winter of 2005/6 left us with only thirty-four sets of legs on the farm, of which seventeen sets belonged to cows, three to the heifers I had chosen to keep (Ladies Olga, Pete and Rebecca) and who had had their first experience of the bull, and thirteen to the previous autumn's calves. The remaining legs belonged to Lady Barbara who, as we found out later, was unable to bear calves and who, after several attempts both with different bulls and AI, we had to let go. This made the work of the rest of the winter reasonably easy. Once the bull had been returned home, we brought the cows and calves back to Eastside and that only left Heinz and Yoghurt as a second group, living in the old cattle shed and grazing the paddocks. By April these numbers were reduced further by the loss of Lady Barbara and the three oldest cows that had not been to the bull. Their calves were now old enough not to need their mothers any more and so once more we had the sadness of seeing them go.

Life was therefore a bit less hectic. I was studying hard and just ventured forth on shopping trips and to see Mother. It was on one of my visits in April to see her at Carlingwark House that I found her unwell. She had always been prone to chest infections and had always had to be careful to nurse any cold she got or else it would get on her chest and she would be quite ill. This day the cold she had been suffering from for several days appeared to be getting worse and, although she would never go to bed, it was clear that she was a poorly lady. The doctor had been called in that morning and had prescribed antibiotics and before I left I managed to persuade her to let the carers put her to bed. That evening we had just finished dinner, when I received a call from the Care manager at Carlingwark House to say that her condition had deteriorated dramatically over the late afternoon and she thought that I should go down and see her for myself. I got the impression that her opinion was that Mother might not last the night and they needed to consult with me over their course of action. Hospitalisation was mentioned as an option. I got in the car and hurried down to Castle Douglas.

I found Mother obviously very ill. She was in bed, extremely comfortable, but pale and breathless. I had no experience of illness and death and so had to be guided by the views of the carers who had obviously seen much in their careers. I asked their candid opinion of what the next hours might bring and they were both of the clear opinion that it was quite possible that she would not live until the morning. I looked at her pale face lying on the pillow and knew that there was no way I wanted her to be taken into hospital. She had always had the happy knack of making those around her love her for her strength of mind, her Yorkshire sense and straight talking and her ability to show everyone the same affection and acceptance. I knew that the people in Carlingwark were no exceptions and that their love and care would surround her that night as she slipped away. She had just celebrated her ninety-fourth birthday and her life had been long and happy with little serious illness and I felt that, if she died that night, surrounded by their care, free of pain and in a very comfortable and by now familiar environment, none of us could have any regrets and it would be a fitting end to her life. I sat with her for a while until she went to sleep and then I said a silent goodbye and drove sadly home to Richard. I had asked the carers to call me if anything happened during the night and felt I could do no more.

There was no phone call and so when I got up early the next morning I rang them. I was only mildly surprised by their answer to my enquiry. 'Oh,' the girl said, 'At four o'clock, she suddenly sat up and asked for a cup of tea!'

I visited each day for the next few days and although she was obviously not well, she insisted on getting up and sitting in the chair and gradually she recovered from the pneumonia that the doctor had diagnosed. I had kept my brothers and my daughter informed daily of her progress, but it was too difficult for any of them to come up to Castle Douglas to see her. My eldest brother lives in Canada, my other brother's wife had a very demanding job in Birmingham, as had my daughter and I began to realise that, having taken her to Scotland to be near me, which was the most important consideration really, I had also prevented her from seeing very much of these other members of her family. David in Canada came over to see her each year, and it made no difference to him where she was, as he could visit Scotland equally as well as Yorkshire, but Philip and my daughter Catherine in the Midlands had only made the journey north once or twice, as their other commitments kept them at home. Until she had become too frail to travel, Richard and I had taken her back to Yorkshire to see her sister and these other family members met us there for lunch, but now these trips were no longer possible. This near death experience was something of a wake-up call for me and I began to think around the problem. Now that Mother was in a care home and unable to do any of the things that she had enjoyed in her previous life, all she needed was to be looked after and to see her family. It didn't seem to matter where she lived, as long as these conditions were fulfilled.

When she was fully recovered, I spoke to her about the matter and she confirmed that these were her only requirements now and that as long as she could be assured that I would still be there to see to her problems and reassure her that all was well, she could be happy anywhere. She also said that it would be good to see more of Catherine and Philip.

My next move was to go down to Leamington Spa where Catherine was now happily living with her handsome American fireman, Morgan, to discuss my embryonic idea with them. This idea was to move Mother to a residential home in Warwick or Leamington and for me to travel down on a very regular basis to see her. It would also mean that I would see more of Catherine and several friends who, by coincidence, lived in the area too. It depended on Catherine's willingness to share the responsibility for overseeing Mother whilst I was in Scotland. I thought that I could manage to get down for at least one week every month, leaving her and my brother the remaining weeks to visit. It was a big ask for a girl who had a very responsible job as a Forensic Scientist, which entailed travelling to Birmingham every day and sometimes working very long hours. I was very prepared for her and Morgan to say it would be too much, even though Catherine had always had a very close relationship with my Mother, having been the only grandchild living nearby. I had gone back to my teaching career when Catherine was nine months old, working three mornings a week, and Mother had looked after her at that time. This had led to them becoming good friends, as well as fostering an excellent grandmother/granddaughter relationship which had grown and flourished through the years.

I wanted Catherine and Morgan to think carefully about the project. Morgan had proposed to Catherine the previous year and their wedding was planned for June 10th. I was visiting them several times in the weeks before the wedding to help with the plans and I broached the subject of moving Mother on one of these trips. I asked them to think about it until my next visit, but they were both clear that this wasn't necessary. Catherine would be pleased to repay her grandmother's care of her and Morgan would support her all he could and so we put the proposal to my brother in Birmingham and he was very much in agreement too. Because of the proximity of the wedding, we decided to leave actually doing anything about the move until the wedding was over and they were back from their honeymoon.

Richard and I continued to talk around the subject, though, and decided that the best thing was for us to buy a place in the area for me to stay in on my future frequent visits to Leamington, rather than impose myself on Catherine and Morgan so often. I began to search the internet for likely places. I needed somewhere in which I would feel safe and which was near enough to reach Catherine's house for short calls, instead of having to make long journeys each time. The whole idea was very attractive and seemed to have benefits for everybody. I had friends in the area and family in Derby, just an hour away by car and it was also near enough to be able to visit friends I had left behind in Yorkshire more regularly than from Scotland. Richard is very self-sufficient and happy with life at the farm and had no objection to me leaving him for short but frequent stays down in England.

My internet search was very short and the first apartment I found looked very suitable. It was in a block of apartments for the over 55s, situated on the Warwick-Leamington road and the photographs on the website made it look attractive. On my next visit south Morgan took me to view it and I fell in love with it straight away. The building is different to the normal square box format of flats and its setting, well back from the busy road, with views towards Warwick Castle across tree filled gardens from one of the living room windows and the grassy entrance to St. John's Park through the opposite one. There are twenty-one apartments set in blocks of four, each with its own entrance, and the one for sale was on the first/top floor in the middle block. It was perfect for my needs and big enough with its second bedroom for visitors. Richard was able to see it when he accompanied me south for the wedding and agreed that it would be a good buy. Our luck did not end there, either. The gentleman who had lived in the flat previously, had left for life in a residential home, but had only been there for two weeks when he died. The flat was still full of his furniture and I agreed for the family to leave any of his things that they did not want. The consequence was that I only had to provide two new pillows for my first stay, as even the bed was new, having been bought for the spare room and never used. I found there enough pots and pans, TV, stereo, sofa, everything in fact that was necessary to begin living there straightaway.

We would complete negotiations to buy the flat whilst we were down in England for the wedding, and then just have to wait for the respective solicitors to do their work, which would take about twelve weeks.

Ten days before the wedding, I went down to Castle Douglas to see Mother and talk to her once more about these plans. She was still sure that she would be happy to move and said that we should carry on with the arrangements. On my return to the car, I found the door very stiff to open. I gave it two or three pulls to no avail and so I yanked hard. The door flew open and impacted on my forehead just above my hairline and for a moment stars whirled around my field of vision. A passer by stopped to see if I was alright and helped me into the driving seat where I sat for a few moments rubbing my head, until I felt safe enough to drive.

On the way home, I thought to myself how fortunate that the impact had been above my hairline so that any resulting bruising would be hidden from view under my bride's mother's hat. I had purchased a beautiful cherry pink and beige outfit in Carlisle and it included hat, shoes and bag to match.

The next morning I searched my image in the mirror for any sign of evidence from the blow and was surprised but very pleased to see no difference in my face to the previous morning. My head was still sore to the touch but unmarked. I put the incident out of my mind and got on with the preparations for leaving the farm to go to the wedding. No one was actually going to come and stay for the five days we would be away, we had just arranged for Linda Corsan to come and feed the cats and Graham would check the animals every day, but they were happily grazing the plentiful grass and would not miss their daily ration until we returned. We planned to take the opportunity to carry on from Leamington and visit an uncle and aunt of Richard's in Abingdon before wending our way back home. Altogether we would be gone for five days.

The incident with the car door was almost forgotten amid all the packing and other preparations, when, on the Sunday morning, just six days before my role as bride's mother was due to take place, I looked in the mirror to see a panda looking back at me. Both my eyes were encircled with thick, black bruising. On one eye the blackness extended from half way across my eyelid, around the outside corner of the eye and right along to my nose. On the other side of my face, the blackness surrounded the eye and extended downwards at the side of my nose. I was horrified!

I called Catherine and wailed to her down the phone. She said that her beautician was coming to do her make up on the morning of the wedding and she would ask her to cover up my black eyes with make up. She could not see them, and I could! It would take many layers of pan stick (remember them?) to provide the cover I needed and I doubted if anything could do more than pay lip service to disguise. I practised with the meagre contents of my make up bag but nothing I had would go anywhere near the coverage required.

The blackness continued to increase in intensity, though not in area, over the next days but by the Saturday morning it was beginning to yellow around the edges. Rosina, the beautician, came and did her best to paint over the hideous bruises with her more comprehensive range of foundation creams, but she could not eliminate them altogether.

With my glasses on and my hat pulled well down over my eyes, I was able to fulfil my role at the church with some confidence and hope that the photographs would not be spoilt. But at the reception, when I had to remove my hat I did not want to have any photographs taken. This was a great shame, as one does not get to be the bride's mother every day.

13
The Wedding

I mentioned previously my mother's Yorkshire sense, which was one of her greatest assets and I am happy to say that she has passed this on to her granddaughter by the bucket load. When it came to planning the wedding, Catherine was determined to have a lovely day, but that it would not cost money that she didn't have. She achieved this admirably. Because neither she nor Morgan had been responsible for the breakdown of their previous marriages, they were granted permission to get married in church, and furthermore in the church of their choice at Burton Dassett in Warwickshire. They had spent much of their courtship in Burton Dassett Country Park and it was here that Morgan had made his very romantic proposal to her the previous year. They were both delighted that they were able to say their vows in this beautiful old country church that meant so much to them. The date was set for June 10th 2006. With Morgan being American and Catherine not a football fan, they did not notice that this was the day of the opening match of England's 2006 World Cup campaign and they had to listen to a few grumbles from their friends, but in the end Catherine made use of this fact. She had decided to have her friend Anna's two little boys as bridesboys, instead of having bridesmaids, as all her close friends were by now married themselves. These two little boys were bedecked in the England football strip, one with her name printed on the back and one with Morgan's name. In place of flowers they each carried a football! This was a bit risky as the boys were only aged 5 and 2 and the balls did get bounced around the church a little, but no-one seemed to mind too much.

Morgan is a fire fighter based in Banbury, and was to be married in full dress uniform. His best friend and best man, Paul is also a fire fighter in Stratford and he too wore his uniform. The firemen colleagues of Morgan's watch were ushers and the sight of so many handsome young men in their smart black suits with white piping and their white helmets enabled us all to feel so proud of them and what they achieve in their daily lives.

None of Morgan's family came over from America for the wedding but a video was being made of the day and Morgan and Catherine were taking this with them when they jetted off to Las Vegas on their honeymoon, the next week. Morgan's father lives near the Grand Canyon and operates a white water rafting company on the Colorado river and his mother was living not far from Las Vegas in Prescott, Arizona at that time and so they would all be able to see the video, as the whole family were gathering for a celebration whilst the happy couple were over there. In spite of the absence of Morgan's family and the small number of Catherine's, the large church was filled with friends, Forensic Scientists and firemen and the lack of family was not an issue at all.

The fire service have maintained a 1952 fire engine for use on ceremonial occasions and Catherine arrived at the church in this ribbon bedecked red appliance, with her bridesboys and their mother. She looked beautiful in the dress she had chosen in Debenham's wedding boutique and which she had waited to buy until their January sale reduced it to half price. She had chosen a white dress and wine red roses with dark green stems for her bouquet and these colours were echoed in all the accessories of the day. She had found a tiara, necklace and earring set of white and dark red stones on ebay and these shone and sparkled in her hair and ears and at her throat. The church was decorated with three large displays of dark red roses and greenery and the service was videoed and photographed by her best friends. It was a beautiful day, and the sun shone on us from early morning until it set late in the evening. This was great for the bride and the guests, but by the end of the service and the photograph session at the church door, poor Morgan and his firemen colleagues were visibly wilting under their thick black serge! Once the photographs were taken, however, they were able to take off their helmets and tunics and looked a lot more comfortable. Morgan and Catherine were once more transported the five miles to the reception in the old fire engine and we followed behind in our cars.

The reception was to be held in the village hall where Catherine and Morgan live. The hall is very small, but there is a large grassy field behind it and Catherine had arranged for a marquee to be erected the previous day and Richard and I and their close friends had all converged on the village to decorate the marquee and prepare some of the food. The worry that the marquee and its preparations could be sabotaged by yobos during the night was solved by the groom, best man and friends staying in it overnight. They did take sleeping bags but I doubt there was much sleep!

The main meal was a barbecue provided by a commercial company and a bar was also provided, but we were called upon to decorate the hall and marquee, chop up large water melons and create the 'wedding cake'. In keeping with the budget projection and in honour of the American connection, Catherine and her friend Clare created a large four tier cake stand from plaster board circles. Edging of strong white satin ribbon was stuck around the raw edge of plaster and then the circles were filled with chocolate and blueberry muffins, each one with two small flags, the Union Jack and the Stars and Stripes, stuck in the top. I had filled small, dark red muslin bags with love hearts and little messages and these were placed alongside the cake.

The reception line took quite a time to greet everyone and, as I was placed at the head of the line, I found myself asking each guest, 'Friend, Forensic or Fire?' as they filed in. They each introduced themselves to me and I was able to put faces to the names Catherine and Morgan had spoken to me about so often and then introduce them to Richard next to me and turn ready to ask the question of the next person. Nobody seemed to bother about my black eyes and soon I forgot about them too and just enjoyed the day.

When everybody had been greeted, we all passed through the hall and out onto the field where the barbecue was being prepared. Everyone cooled off first with the large slices of watermelon and soon we were eating the lamb steaks, beef burgers and salad from the food preparation area at the far side of the field. For a dessert, Catherine had arranged for the local ice cream man to call at the field at 7pm and we were alerted to his perfectly timed arrival by his jingling tune just as the hot food was finished. Everyone chose whatever they wanted from the van and those that liked the sun sat around in groups on the grass and the others sat in the shade of the marquee licking cornets and lollies.

Once the eating was over, it was time for the speeches. Anyone who knows fire fighters will know that the way they cope with the horrors they see so often in their job, is to perpetrate sometimes outrageous jokes on each other and Morgan was a little apprehensive, knowing full well that something would have been prepared by the other members of his watch for him on this special day. However, he needn't have worried, for when it came it was to give us all the best kind of laugh. After the normal speeches of the best man, groom and bride's father had been made and the usual toasts drunk, the Leading Fireman of White Watch appeared on the stage carrying a very large parcel. 'Well, Morgan,' he began, 'we couldn't let this day pass without showing how much we appreciate your membership of our happy band of firemen. You have driven us all mad over the last year or two with your very narrow topics of conversation. If you weren't talking about how wonderful Catherine is, which we all know anyway, you were banging on about your golfing prowess, and so we are presenting you with this gift as a reminder of your sport and hope that it will help you to get over the fact that you couldn't play today!' He then presented the large parcel to Morgan. Inside the paper wrapping was a large box and from this Morgan pulled a very old and tatty golf bag. As he opened this, someone shouted, 'It's a new set of irons, Morgan!' From the bag, he pulled seven brand new household irons, each bearing the Tesco value brand and each inscribed in large letters with the name of a famous golfing manufacturer on their box. The marquee erupted in laughter and applause.

The bride then continued the rather unorthodox procedures of the day by giving a long and amusing speech aimed principally at her long standing friends and her family who had all attended her first wedding some six years previously. She thanked us all for bearing with her through the bad times that had resulted in the breakdown of that marriage and apologised to those of us whom she had told that she wouldn't be repeating the exercise, as clearly she had reneged on that promise. She ended by declaring what was so plain for all to see, by reading to him a poem that she had written, funny in places but nonetheless very sincere, that she had truly found in Morgan the love of her life.

The dancing then started and as darkness began to overtake the summer sky, slowly people began to drift away home, taking with them their memories of a really joy filled and successful day.

The wedding ended later that night with the groom unceremoniously hoisting the bride in a fireman's lift and marching up the village to their little house, where he carried her over their very happy threshold!

Catherine and Mother

Waiting in the snow for breakfast

Richard obliges

The bride arrives at the church in the old fire engine

The bride surrounded by Morgan and his firemen colleagues

Leaving for the reception in the fire engine

The marquee awaits the wedding guests

The 'wedding cake'

Eve Chouette

By the Aga (Reproduced by kind permission of George Carrick)

Richard fit and well again with Linda and the Ladies
(Reproduced by kind permission of George Carrick)

The new shed is ready ......

.....and occupied

Henry back in his favourite chair

David is not too sure about things

The Ladies arrive in Poland

Lady Isla and the first Polish calf

Settled and happy in Poland

14

Autumn 2006

The summer progressed in an unremarkable fashion at Low Arvie. Getting the grass cut and making the silage for the next winters feed is always the most stressful time for us because of the Galloway weather. We need at least three consecutive days without rain .The grass has to be mown and then left for a time, preferably in sunshine, to wilt and dry out as much as possible before it is baled and wrapped in its plastic 'cling film' jacket. Since our first years' efforts to buy and operate our own machinery for this process had ended in the disasters catalogued in my previous annal, we are now reliant upon finding contractors to come and do these jobs for us. When the weather is uncertain, everybody in the area has to take advantage of any good spells and this makes it difficult to arrange for the contractors to come to us. We only have a small amount of good grassland to cut and this is very hilly and can be dangerous for large tractors when the ground is wet and slippery. Also most farms in the area are much bigger than ours and the contractors all have their long standing customers to service, who obviously take precedence over us. Now that we have been at Low Arvie for seven years we have managed to build up a good relationship with a couple of contractors in the area who do their best to fit us in but the early years were quite difficult in this respect. Tom Corsan will always do his best to come and mow the grass but then we have to find a baler and wrapper man who can follow on from Tom two days later. Once the grass is baled and wrapped, the bales then have to be carried back to the farm one at a time and stacked in their compound. The whole process is long and laborious and if the rain comes before this is all finished, the carting has to be stopped as the Matbro handler which Richard uses to do this job is a very heavy machine, which slips and slides in the mud and leaves long brown scars across the fields.

Until 2008, we belonged to the Rural Stewardship Scheme, which paid us a subsidy to leave the grass mowing until after the first of July to enable the nesting birds to get their families raised and on their feet in the long grass. We found that this exacerbated the grass problem even further, because July is often a very wet month. In the five years that we were in the scheme, no birds ever nested in our grass fields and so now we have left the scheme and are free to cut the grass towards the end of June if the weather allows. Clearly the accounts suffer greatly from the loss of the grant, but stress levels are much reduced.

We chose our calving time to fit into the pattern of this grass cutting timetable because we needed the cows to calve in the grassy silage fields rather than the rough pasture. The Galloway mothers are very protective in the earliest days of their calf's life and they hide them in the rushes. It is impossible to find them without the most diligent searching, which, of course, is the point of this hiding process, but Richard has to tag them and, also, he needs to see them every day to be sure that they are well and are suckling. It is much easier to achieve this if the cows are in the grassy areas which have less rush growth. This part, then, of our farming life is like a big jigsaw in which we have to fit all the pieces together in the correct way. The cows need a month or two away from their previous calf to 'dry off' and prepare to give birth again, and so the ideal scenario in the scheme years was to make the silage in early July, leave the silage fields empty for a week or two to allow the grass to put on some more growth, then wean last year's calves and put the mothers into the grass fields around the beginning of August ready for their next calving in September and October. The bull would then make his appearance in late November to create the next year's progeny.

It is clear, then, that rain in July was the worst thing that could occur. Delaying the silage making which was of prime importance, pushed all the other pieces of the jigsaw back, hence the stress that was caused at this time of the year.

We were still in the scheme in 2006, but the weather was kind and we managed to mow the grass in the second week of July and the cows were all in their correct places when Lady Rebecca produced the first calf of that year on August 31st. The other calves followed over the next few weeks and by the time the men came to erect the shed in October, all the summer work had progressed in good order.

In the preceding weeks, we had completed the purchase of the flat in Warwick and I moved myself and my two pillows in on September 26th. As I had hoped, it is the most perfect place for my trips down to England. Catherine lives just eight miles away and we are able to follow a very happy mother/daughter lifestyle in the weeks I am in Warwick, without having to share the same space and living arrangements. I can pop in for coffee and a chat whenever convenient, and with Morgan's work as a fireman meaning that he spends two nights in every eight on duty at the fire station, we also have lots of time to go out together or just to pass evenings in quality mother and daughter time. I am invited to lots of meals at their house, which are usually made by Morgan, who is an excellent cook and has time to make them when he is not at work. I also see my cousins, Gaye and Geraldine, in Derby on almost every visit and have rekindled the wonderful relationship we had when we spent our teenage years together back in the 1960s. This has given me so much happiness and is just one of the added dimensions that the flat in Warwick has added to my life. There are also other friends that I knew during my school days who, by coincidence, live around the area and whom I am able to see on a very regular basis. There is no doubt that it is nice to make new friends, but, for me, it is these re-found old ones who enrich my life.

When Catherine and Morgan returned from their honeymoon in America, they had set about finding a care home in the area for Mother. After looking at a few that they could not recommend, they went to see Clarendon Manor at Whitnash, just outside Leamington Spa. Catherine rang to tell me about it and said that they had both liked it very much and thought that Mother would be fine there. It is situated just about five miles from Catherine's house and three from the flat. I came down from Scotland and went with my brother, Philip, to look at it. We agreed with Catherine and Morgan's assessment. Luckily there was a room available and so I went home and told Mother all about it and started the process of getting her moved. Mother has always made my promised task of looking after her in her old age so easy. She has always trusted that all my decisions made on her behalf have been made with her best interests at heart. Her only request throughout the years since my father died has been that I should always be there to save her worries and solve her problems. I can honestly say that I have done this and it has been a pleasure to do it.

She was by now 94 years old, but she faced this new move to an unknown destination with the same positive attitude that she showed when I took her to Scotland in 2002. Richard and I collected her and her now few possessions from Carlingwark House early on October 8th and we met my brother at the Charnock Richard service station on the M6. Mother and I continued south with him, while Richard returned home to the farm. We arrived at Clarendon Manor just in time for lunch and, whilst Mother enjoyed a roast lamb dinner, we took her things into her room and personalized it as much as we could for her. The room was quite small but had all the necessary fitments and, by the time we left, it was cosy and hers.

I returned later that evening with Catherine and we found her comfortably installed in the large lounge with some of the other residents. I am pleased to say that the move to Leamington worked out wonderfully for Mother. The home was much livelier than Carlingwark and Mother soon settled into a regime which suited her much better. The night staff took her a cup of tea when she woke and then got her up and dressed ready for her preferred early breakfast. She then spent the day in the lounge where she was befriended by a lady called Tilly, who became an excellent companion, watching over Mother and helping her to settle in. The members of staff were all long standing employees of the home and we soon came to be assured that they all had the best interests of their charges at heart. Mother came to be loved by them all and, being the oldest resident and one of the least demanding, she was soon known to all of them as 'Grandma', a term they used in great affection. She was so pleased to be able to see Catherine and Philip on a regular basis and I got into a routine of spending every third week in Warwick, when I visited her every day. While I was in Scotland, Catherine went to see her three times a week and we began to see a change occurring in Mother's state of mind. She became much livelier and the deterioration in her short term memory seemed to halt and I am very clear in my mind that the move south was the best thing that we could have achieved for her.

I have never found it easy to deal with the personal care of other people but Catherine's early years of working as a Forensic Scientist in the Drugs department meant that she had to open and analyse drug packages which had been transported to this country in many strange places, usually contained in the various apertures of the human body. These experiences have left her immune to working with the many secretions that come from such places and she now was able to share in coping with the personal needs of her Grandmother without any problems. Mother's weekly bath took place on Thursday evenings and Catherine made it in her way to visit at this time and oversee the care of her skin, which was becoming ever more frail and delicate. One Thursday at work, a colleague asked Catherine what her plans for the evening were. 'Oh, it's Thursday,' she replied, 'so tonight I shall be moisturizing Grandma!'

The years spent in Leamington Spa greatly enhanced the quality of Mother's last years and I am so grateful to Catherine for all the care and love that she gave to us both during that time. Also, I am thankful that Morgan provided her with all the support that she needed and I came to know that sharing this difficult time of watching a much loved parent approach the end of her life with others who care as much and in the same way makes it so much easier to bear.

15

Another wall problem

With most of the calves born and running about and the shed project on hold for the winter, Richard felt able to take a well deserved day off from the farm in November and went with a farmer friend to the AgriScot exhibition near Edinburgh. I didn't go with him but stayed at home and, when he had gone, I decided to do some baking. This is not my most favourite occupation but when I have the time to myself, I can usually produce reasonably edible offerings.

I was just up to my elbows in flour making a batch of scones when the telephone rang. I contemplated not answering it and letting the answer phone do it for me, but I am not very good at doing this and so I wiped some of the flour off my hands and picked up the receiver. It was Dorothy from Auchenvey. She and Willie had just been up to look at their sheep and on returning down the hill across the road had discovered that two large gaps had appeared in the dry stone wall the separated our Auchenvey field from the road. She reported to me that there was no-one in sight but that the cows and calves were fast approaching the gaps to investigate. Auchenvey field is at the far end of the farm next to Dorothy and Willie's Auchenvey farm and it is about half a mile along the road from Low Arvie farmhouse. The field is split into two halves by a dry stone wall that we had had repaired, but with the cows and calves using the field as their winter quarters, the two gates in this wall had been left open to give them the whole area for grazing. Dorothy said that the gaps in the road wall were each about three metres wide and ten metres apart and were in the larger western half of the field. The only vehicle that I could drive was winging its way to Edinburgh with Richard and Graham McQuaker and so I had no alternative but to don coat and wellies and get up there on my two feet as fast as I could. I did just take a minute to make an SOS call to Tom at Arvie and Linda, his wife, said that he would soon be in for his lunch and she would ask him to come and help as soon as possible.

Exercise of any kind is not my forte and I puffed and panted my way up the road as quickly as I could, all the time fearing that I would meet our Galloways coming the other way, or even worse that I would arrive at the field to see them disappearing in the distance the other way. I was relieved, therefore, to see some black heads on the other side of the dividing wall as I neared the field gate. I began to call Beauty, hoping that she would find her way to me in the nearest side of the field and bring the rest of the herd with her. I might then be able to shut the gates in the wall enclosing them in the smaller eastern part of the field where they would be safe until Richard could see to the mending of the wall. How I thanked my lucky stars for Beauty's intelligence that day, because long before I had reached the gate into the field, she came to my calls through to the east side and there behind her were, as far as I could tell, all the rest of the cows with their calves beside them. Now all I had to do was to squelch my way to the two gates and close them before Beauty discovered that my approach didn't mean anything in the way of a treat for her, like a bucket of cake, and take everybody back to investigate the more interesting holes in the wall. I knew that this would be a lot easier said than done because the ground was very wet and soggy and I had to cross the area where Richard gave them their daily ration. Here the mud, mixed with the cows'. frequent deposits, was thick and sticky and would grab a welly in a vice like grip. If you were hurrying across this ground too quickly, the welly would stick in the mud and you could easily find yourself taking the next steps in your stocking feet. The gates that needed closing are at least a hundred metres apart and the ground between them was rough and undulated severely in several places. It would be a tricky task to achieve and I was verging on desperation as I got near to the entrance gate into West Auchenvey.

My mind was fully occupied with thoughts of the next minutes in which I hoped to ensure the safety of our animals and I was only dimly aware of the approach of a smallish Fiat car around the corner. My eyes saw its dirty battered bonnet and the streaks of mud along its side, and also the long length of dayglo orange tape that appeared to be holding the bonnet on the car in its approximately correct position, but I did not at first realise its significance to my present position. I was just about to enter the field when the car pulled up alongside me and peering through the side window, I saw the extremely cheerful face of the young man who was driving, and the countless papers and articles of office equipment strewed around him like the stall at a jumble sale. 'Is this your field?' he asked me. When I answered in the affirmative, he said, 'I was looking for the owner, but drove the other way to the next farm. They told me to come back this way. I have to tell you that I have made rather a mess of your wall.' I told him that I had been informed of this, and he continued, 'I lost control of the car going round the bend and I hit the wall with the front end of the car.' 'Hence the tape holding the bonnet on', I thought. 'Then the car spun round and I crashed into the wall further along with the rear end,' he continued. 'Hence the second gap in the wall,' I thought. 'But don't worry. It's a company car and I have rung my office for the insurance details and I was just bringing them to you.' He wrote the name, address and telephone number on one of the pieces of paper that littered the interior of the car, and then he added his own name and telephone number and handed the paper to me through the window.

Throughout this conversation, I had attempted to pay attention to the young man, whilst keeping an eye on Beauty in the field, and once I had the paper, I didn't detain the man and he went on his way with the orange streamers flowing behind him.

The cows had come up to the road gate to see what I was doing and I was thankful that their curiosity had centred on me. My first goal was to close the nearest gate in the dividing wall and I managed to achieve this whilst keeping the cattle on the correct side of it. Now for the hard part and I set off across the quagmire of the feeding ground towards the lower gate. My progress was slowed by the mud as I had expected, but happily my wellies stayed on my feet as I slipped and slithered along. Once I reached the rough grass, the going was just as hard and I struggled along as quickly as I could up and down the rushy, stony ground. Beauty followed me for a while but then she lost interest, presumably realising that there was no bucket in sight, and she went back to the other cows who, with nothing more to take their interest for the moment, had gone back to their grazing. It was a long way to the second gate, but eventually I made it and breathed a sigh of relief as I closed it behind them. I then set off across the now empty western half of the field to inspect the damage, but as I got around the first knoll I saw that the field was not empty. There by the holes in the wall were Linda and Tom, carrying between them a long gate, with which they were blocking up most of the nearest hole. By them, up on the road, I could see Dorothy and Willy. Linda and Tom must have passed by in their car whilst I was talking to the young man and Dorothy had met them and offered them two gates to close off the gaps. They had fetched them and had already put one across the smaller hole that was closer to Auchenvey farm.

Once again, we had cause to be grateful for the kindness of this farming community in coming to our rescue. The gates remained in place whilst we were sorting out the mending of the wall with the insurance company, thus allowing the cattle to have their full amount of grazing all the time. I was also thankful that the young man was more honest than the girl who had punctured our wall the previous year, as the bill for mending the two holes in the wall was quite considerable, and I hope that he managed to get his car fixed and didn't suffer any ill effects from his experience.

16

Studies and Belties

My studies for this second year of my degree quest had culminated in my taking two exams. My main effort had been put into the Biology course as this had all been new knowledge for me, whereas I had found the Latin to be quite easy. This latter course was aimed at people who were starting to learn this wonderful language without having any previous experience of it, whereas I had learned to love it in my days at Grammar School back in the sixties. I found the assignments easy to complete and had been able to concentrate most of my efforts on learning about the workings of the human body. I became fascinated with the section about our immune system and discovered the marvellous ways in which this system works to fight the invading army of bacteria and viruses by which we are constantly bombarded. Our bodies are constantly playing our very own space invaders game and the complicated but beautifully crafted way in which we tilt the odds in our favour against an enemy that is constantly providing itself with new weapons of attack is truly marvellous. Of course, this was only one part of the biological knowledge that I was trying to acquire in order to regurgitate some of it in answer to the examination questions and I felt very nervous as the exam day approached. As expected, the Latin exam caused me no great problems and I expected that I would be able to achieve a high grade in that one, but I was thrilled to pieces when I got my results in December to discover that I had achieved a Distinction in Biology as well. The grade awarded takes account of the marks received in the assignments as well as the examination and to get this grade across both of these sections in a subject that was so new to me was something of which I felt I could be justifiably proud. These courses were both at level 2 and worth 30 points each. I had already completed my 120 points at level 1 with a 10 point Mathematics course and so was now half way to my goal.

I had continued to study the Spanish course with Jan throughout the year and decided that, having had this extra time of study for it, I would register to do this 60 point course myself to complete my level 2 points in the next year and, at the same time, set out on gaining those I needed at level 3. It seemed obvious that I should carry on with the 30 pointer Continuing Classical Latin, but I knew that this would need more time than I had needed to give to the earlier Latin course. My trips down to Warwick to see my Mother and spend time with Catherine had proved to be beneficial to my studies as well, giving me hours of train travel and quite a lot of spare time at the flat and so I felt that, with the Spanish half done and my previous Latin knowledge, I could afford to register for a second 30 point level 3 course as well. Looking through the prospectus, I spied the very thing. There was a course named Infectious Disease, which concentrated on the immune system response to disease and would take my level 2 learning of this to a deeper level. I had no hesitation in registering for all three courses and prepared myself for a hard year of study. I had become familiar enough with the work that I did for the farm, keeping the accounts and the farm records up to date, and I felt that this wouldn't suffer too much, whilst I concentrated my efforts on studying. If I passed the three courses, I would have the 300 points required for an ordinary degree and would be entitled to put the coveted letters BSc after my name, although I would have to continue for a further year to convert this ordinary degree into Honours. My goal was to achieve a First Class Honours degree, but the standard for this in the OU is very high, requiring passes at 85% or higher in both assignments and examinations and I knew that, now the levels were higher, this would be difficult to achieve in such disparate subjects. I determined to give it my best shot.

The Spanish course required a week's attendance at summer school in

Santiago del Compostela in northern Spain which would take place the following August and I began to discuss with Richard how this could be worked in with the farm. Our plans crystallized into taking five weeks away from the farm and driving down to Barcelona to spend time with the friends we had made during our two winters spent there before coming to Low Arvie, and then driving across Spain to the summer school before wending our way back up through France. This was very ambitious in view of our commitments to our animals but we decided to try and find people who would come to look after things in our absence. If we couldn't do this, then the alternative was for me to fly to Santiago for the week and leave Richard at home, so either way I could fulfil the conditions of the course and I completed the registration forms and began work on my studies.

We hoped to complete the silage before leaving the farm on our trip and this would mean that the cattle would only need to be checked on daily for any problems. There would be very little in the way of arduous work, as the previous year's calves would be weaned and the cows would not yet be ready to calve again until after our return. We spoke to Tom Corsan and asked if he would be able to see to the silage for us, if we couldn't get it done before we left in the middle of July and he said that this would be no problem. We had also found a man called Roy who had come to live just a long the road from us and had lots of farming experience. He was not employed full time and had been called on a few times to come and help Richard with two man tasks. He, too, would be prepared to come and check up on things for us. So it was just a question of finding someone to come and live in the house and have a nice Galloway holiday. Once again, we were very lucky and when some friends visited us one day and we told them of our plans, Diana said that her cousin might be willing to help us out. It was soon fixed up that the cousin's son and his wife would come for two of the five weeks and the cousin, Suzie, and her husband, John, would take the other three. It all seemed as if providence was with us and we began to make our plans in earnest.

The three courses all began in November and so soon I was fully occupied with studying, travelling to Warwick, where Mother was becoming very settled and happy at Clarendon Manor, and my farm work. Eleven calves had been born in the autumn with no problems and no dramas and we were now awaiting with excitement the birth of the two Belted Galloway calves from the cows that had been inseminated. We knew that they were both pregnant and the due dates were in December. Olga was the first to give birth and I was studying in the flat when Richard rang to say that she had had a fine bull calf, but, disappointingly, the only sign of his Beltie heritage was a short white flash on one side. Nevertheless, Olga was thrilled with her first offspring and all was well with them both.

I was once more in Warwick, spending New Year with Catherine and Morgan, when Gina had her calf, a heifer, three weeks later. She was born on New Year's Eve and, what was more, she had a full white belt around her girth. The belt was narrow in places but nevertheless it was there and she would add interest to our herd. The mother, Gina, was named for a friend of ours who kept a beautiful Bed and Breakfast house in northern France, just south of Calais, where we always stayed the first and last nights of our continental trips. When we had told her that she had a calf named after her, Gina had requested that the first heifer calf she produced should be named Chouette, and so we called the calf Eve Chouette. She wasn't a full pedigree and could not be given the title of Lady, as we could not register her, but I thought that Eve Chouette had quite an elegant ring to it and was highly suitable for our first Beltie heifer.

We had been lucky enough to get another bull from Scott, who was now becoming a name to be reckoned with in Black Galloway circles, having won several top prizes with his Klondyke animals in that year's agricultural shows and Klondyke Legend, another son of Blackcraig Gusto, came to Low Arvie to consort with the cows over the winter months.

17

American visitors

The road that forms the southern boundary of the farm is the A712 and it runs from the village of Crocketford on the A75 between Dumfries and Castle Douglas to the village of Balmaclellan and then crosses the A713 and passes through New Galloway and on to Newton Stewart where it connects up again with the A75 to Stranraer. Our stretch from Crocketford to Balmaclellan is about sixteen miles long and Low Arvie is situated just about half way along, a mile and a quarter west of the village of Corsock. There is not a lot of traffic on it but, having no pavement and few houses along its length, we hardly ever see any people walking past the farm at any time.

One Friday morning the next April, I was heating the soup that was to be our lunch and gazing through the kitchen window, when I was surprised to see what looked to me like a tramp plodding slowly past the farm. The weather was cold and we were still waking in the mornings to rime covered fields and feeding cows whose black coats were covered with thick white frost. (The Galloways have a two layer winter coat and are very hardy creatures that do not mind the cold.) Even when they have this white layer on their backs, you can dig your fingers through the hair and find that their bodies are snug and warm beneath. They mainly only use the sheds, which are available to them at all times, to shelter from the heat of the summer sun, which causes them far more distress than the winter cold.

I watched as the figure, huddled beneath layers of coats, scarves and hat made its way slowly past the house, rucksack on back, and arriving at the end of the drive, it sank wearily onto the wall across the road. It was plain that something was wrong. At that moment a second figure came into sight, following the first. This person was walking with more purpose, but still slowly and, as Richard came into the house for his lunch at that moment, I suggested he went down the drive to see what and who they were.

In a little while, he came back up the drive with the two people and brought them into the house. As they unwound the scarves and divested themselves of the many layers of clothing, I saw that they were two women. The elder one, who was the first one I had seen, looked very pale and seemed about to faint. We sat them down at the kitchen table and I poured the soup into two bowls and placed them in front of the ladies. They ate the soup hungrily along with most of a loaf. As they ate, we listened to their story which was quite amazing. They were Americans from Michigan State and the elder one, whose name was Cynthia, had just celebrated her sixtieth birthday. Her friend, Sue, had suggested that they should come to the UK and spend a few weeks backpacking around. They had had no idea that the weather in Scotland would be so cold at this time of year and they had made their way north to Wigtownshire to find Cynthia's family roots. They were obviously quite poor and explained that they had been on their way to Dumfries to pick up some money from the Western Union terminal there which they hoped their family in America had been able to send. They were hoping to get a bus to take them there and had not realised that this form of transport in rural Dumfries and Galloway is not the every twenty minute kind. In fact we only have one bus a day past the farm, at 8 a.m., except on Wednesdays and Saturdays, when a second bus passes at 10a.m. This one returns at 4 p.m. and on other days the returning bus is at 5.30p.m. and these cater for workers and shoppers. This was Friday and so the bus for that day had gone long since.

As their story unfolded, it became clear that these two hapless travellers were in dire straits. Their back packs each held a small one man tent, with an even smaller fly sheet, they had only instant soup and a bar of chocolate as sustenance, no cooking appliance to heat the soup and they were collecting water from the drains and ditches in a small container no bigger than a

Nescafe jar. They were on their way to Norfolk, where they said they had friends who would put them up before they caught their flight back to the US in a month's time.

Cynthia had long grey hair, tied up in a plait, and two tattoos on her face, one of which adorned her cheek and was in the form of a hieroglyph of some kind and the other was a long blue line which began by one ear and traced around her forehead to the other ear. She told us that she was an astrologist and these were astrological symbols. Sue also had tattoos, and these were a kind of permanent jewellery, forming earrings at her earlobes, necklace round her neck and bracelets on her wrists. She was a gemmologist and had a small shop in their home town, where she sold rocks and crystals and Cynthia plied her trade creating astrology charts.

As they talked and ate, the colour came back into their faces and I realised that they had not eaten properly for days and obviously had had nothing warm to drink either. How they came to be tramping along our road remains a mystery which I never solved. When Richard had approached them first, they had told him that they were hoping to find a shop, but as with the buses, these are few and far between along the A712. Corsock village is only possessed of a public house, where Jim and Maretta Pringle serve meals and Jim was, at that time, the post master dispensing pensions and stamps from the small enclosure in one corner of the single public room. Even that service has been closed by Government orders in 2009 and we now have to manage with a van that calls at the village for two hours a week, on Mondays and Thursdays. The only shops along our road are found in Crocketford, 8 miles one way and Balmaclellan 8 miles the other. Our main shopping towns are Castle Douglas 12 miles away and Dumfries 9 miles past Crocketford.

I made more soup for Richard and me and we continued to question our unbidden guests and talk about their problems. The more they talked, the more we realised that these were paramount. They had been camping in their small tents by the roadside, drinking water from the burns and using up their meagre food rations for several days and here they were miles from what they would consider civilization, with very little money and no hope of getting any more until they got to Dumfries

We could not do anything but offer to allow them to stay on the farm overnight and then they could catch the morning bus to Dumfries the next day. Sue said that she wanted to communicate with her daughter back in Michigan and so while she went into the office to do this, I made them a flask of hot water so that, at least they could make a warm drink. Then Richard took them off to find a suitable spot to pitch their tents somewhere on the farm. With the cattle in Eastside and Auchenvey for the summer, they decided that the grass field nearest to the house would be suitable and the wall at the far side would afford them some protection from the cold winds.

We had friends coming for a meal that evening and I needed to get on with preparing the food. The story telling had taken up valuable time and I was now behind in my preparations and so I had to give my attention to this for the next few hours.

Later that afternoon the reply came through from Sue's daughter and, as I read it, it became clear that her email had been asking if the money she had been expecting from some kind of Government benefit had arrived in time to be sent through to Dumfries that day. The reply was not encouraging. The money had not arrived and so nothing had been sent yet but the daughter said she would email again once she had more news. 'What,' I wondered, 'had we got ourselves into?' I printed off the message and went outside. I could see the bright red tents pitched in our Inbye field and I walked up to deliver the email. I was quite surprised to find that, in the intervening time, they had managed to create quite a snug and cosy living space. The two tents were pitched facing the wall in a triangular shape and the empty middle of the triangle was covered over by one of the fly sheets which was then attached to the top of the wall. I peered inside and saw Cynthia sitting cross-legged in the tent, with a few coins spread out on the top of the sleeping bag in front of her. It amounted to £2.32. This it seemed was the full complement of their resources and, with the bus fare to Dumfries priced at £1.60 each, it would not even get them there.

Before our friends came that night, I packed a basket with bread rolls and cheese, apples and biscuits, filled another flask and took it all up to the two wayfarers for their evening meal.

When Amanda and Peter had arrived and were served with their aperitifs, I regaled them with the day's events. Amanda is a very forthright lady and her view of the proceedings was very clear. She laughed at our part in the story and expressed the view that we had saddled ourselves with a very thorny problem. She also warned me not to let our generosity be taken for granted and to lock the doors before we went to bed lest we be murdered while we slept. Of course, she had not met our 'visitors' and had not seen the straits in which they had arrived at our door. She is also a very kind lady who would have done exactly the same as us, but it didn't stop her joking at our expense. We simply had not been able to leave these strangers to our country to an unimaginable fate without money, food or warmth in the cold and frosty weather of a Galloway April, and neither would she.

Before I went to bed, I checked for another message. It said that the money had come through, but that there had been urgent debts that had had to be paid and this had left only $100, which the daughter would send through to Dumfries, but that it would not arrive before the shop closed on Saturday lunch time.

I struggled my way once more through the dark field to deliver the email and said that it was plain that our 'guests' would have to stay until the bus on Monday morning. I realised that, as well as feeding our guests over the weekend, I would also have to give them enough money to make up the requisite amount to get them on this first leg of their journey.

18

Weekend Guests

On the Saturday morning, Sue came down to the farm house and I found her filling the flask with hot water from the tap outside the kitchen wall. I took it from her to fill with boiling water from the kettle and invited her in to discuss their plans further. She was feeling much better and said that Cynthia, also, was in a more comfortable state. She admitted to me that she had been so worried about her over the past few days. Sue was much younger than her companion and had stood up better to the cold weather and the long hours of walking that they had endured. She said that they had arrived in England three weeks earlier and had made their way by public transport as far as Sheffield, where, she said, they had either been robbed of their money or had lost it. They had then received an injection of cash from America and had used it to get to Wigtown where they had looked for Cynthia's forebears. Somehow, from there, they had found their way onto the A712. Her story wasn't very clear in places but my assessment of her was that she was a genuine person who was properly grateful for the help that we had given. After all, it had been freely offered and, frankly, they had not had any other choice but to accept it. She took the flask but refused my offer of more food, saying they had plenty left from my previous basketful and, on her way back to the tents, she made a detour to find Richard in the byre. He later told me that she had begged him to let her do some work to repay our hospitality, but he had declined her offer.

The two ladies spent the day walking round the fields and resting to replenish their strength ready for the next stage of their journey. We were invited out to eat with some friends in Balmaclellan that night and before we left I restocked their larder from my pantry.

When I told Diane and Graham the story, Diane recalled that she had seen the travellers passing their house on the Thursday and had spotted their red tents pitched by the side of the road later in the day. She had debated whether to stop and ask if she could help them, but, in the end, had not done so as commitments for her time were pressing. It was clear from the conversation that they were willing to help where they could and before we left to return home, Graham had offered to pick the Americans up on his way to Dumfries on Monday morning and drop them near the Western Union office. He would be leaving early and asked for the ladies to be ready by 7.45a.m. if they wanted to accept his lift. I promised to phone and let him know the next day. It seemed unlikely that they would refuse, as the time was so near to the time they would need to catch the bus anyway, and it would save their precious money from having to be spent on bus fares.

The next day was Sunday and it was a beautiful spring day, although still very cold. After breakfast, I went up to the campsite, to see how the women were faring and to check on the food situation. I told them of Graham's offer and they did accept it gratefully. They promised to be ready at the appointed time and then, once again, expressed a wish to repay us in some way for the help they had received. Sue said that, on her wanderings around the farm the previous day, she had collected various different coloured stones from the fields and she intended to take them home and polish them. She would then create for Richard a picture of the farm from them. Cynthia promised that she would make our astrological charts, if I gave her our birthdays. They said that this was all they had been able to think of in the way of thanks and asked once again if there was anything else that I could suggest. Sue said that she had begged Richard to find her some kind of work, but he had not been able to think of anything suitable. At that moment, I was inspired to make a suggestion. Neither Richard nor I are gardeners, and once we had cleared the patch of ground in front of the farmhouse during our first year of occupation, we had done little more than cut the lawn and keep things as tidy as we could. Richard mowed the green areas (which were mainly moss and wild flowers rather then actual grass) and it was nominally my job to see to the small areas of supposed flower borders. Since I had begun studying, I must admit that these had been totally neglected and were now overgrown and untidy. We had employed a gardener for a short time the previous year but he had been ill and had only come once or twice before telling us the work was too much for him. I asked Sue how she felt about weeding the untidy sections of the garden and she seemed genuinely delighted and only sorry that she hadn't been given this task the day before, which would have allowed her to do so much more. She immediately set off to find the requisite tools which lay unused and covered in cobwebs in the greenhouse and spent the rest of the day yanking out weeds and chopping back greenery.

I decided to invite the two of them into the house that evening for a warm meal and offer them the use of the shower room to help them to feel more refreshed for the next stage of their journey. While Sue worked away with a will in the garden, Cynthia and I sat and watched and chatted away like old friends. I soon discovered that any initial fears I had had that these two would be a major problem for us had dissolved over the two days that they were with us and I really enjoyed their company and was so glad that we had been able to make a real difference to their lives and their Scottish experience.

The garden certainly benefitted from Sue's efforts and I gained a lot of previously unknown knowledge, both about their respective fields and about life in America. They appeared at the dinner table that night refreshed and relaxed and we all enjoyed a happy evening together, before they left once more to sleep in their tents.

The next morning at 7.30a.m., they appeared at the backdoor, once more garbed in their layers of clothing, scarves and hats. Cynthia had no gloves and she explained that she had lost them along the way. I fetched a pair of my thick woollen ones from the drawer in the kitchen and, with this parting gift, they set off to the end of the drive to await Graham's lift. He came along promptly at 7.45a.m., and, after installing their backpacks in the boot of his car, he presented them with a cake which Diane had sent for their journey. We hugged our goodbyes and they disappeared down the road to Dumfries.

Towards the end of the next week, we received a postcard from them. They had managed to pick up their meagre injection of cash and were presently living in a caravan they had rented on a campsite in the Lake District. They once again thanked us for our help and promised to get in touch once they were home.

We did have an email from Cynthia saying that the rest of their time in England had been quite uneventful and that they had made it back to the States safely. It seemed that while they had been away, the premises that they used for their work had been repossessed and things were once more difficult for them. They had both been forced to take menial jobs to make ends meet. We never received our astrological charts or the polished stone picture, but we have the memories of a very interesting weekend spent with two people from a very different environment from ours and, given the same circumstances, I would not hesitate to do the same thing again.

This was not my only contact with Americans that year for, a few weeks later, I was once again in the kitchen, when I spotted that a car had drawn up in the entrance to our drive and a man was wandering around, apparently aimlessly, from one side of the drive to the other. I went out to see what he was about and I approached and asked if I could help him. I could see a lady sitting in the car and wondered if they had broken down. 'Oh, no', he drawled in a Southern States accent, 'I just stopped by to look at your waaalls. I'm just fascinated by your waaalls'. I once more took the opportunity to pass time with interesting people and invited them into the house for a cup of coffee. They stayed an hour and took away with them a copy of 'The Ladies of Low Arvie' to read about our story and the life we lead, which is so different to theirs.

I love these 'ships that pass in the night' interludes which leave each participant enriched by the other and I take any opportunity that offers to learn about people and places unknown. I have rarely found them to be anything other than interesting and informative and one never knows where they might lead.

19

The Dales Diary

As the days grew longer, the trees began to take on the first tinges of springtime green. This is my favourite time of the year, and in Dumfries and Galloway it is especially enjoyable because the weather warms up more slowly than in the south and the spring takes longer to arrive. This is the only time that the garden in front of the farmhouse looks truly beautiful. When we went to the farm, one of our first jobs was to clear the weeds which covered practically the whole of the garden and this long and boring task was rewarded early that first spring when we discovered a huge patch of snowdrops growing amongst the green moss and grass. It was even better when, a few weeks later, we saw the green shoots of wild daffodil leaves began to appear amongst the dying snowdrops. These are my very favourite flowers and they cover a patch of about ten square yards. As well as these, we found large clumps of cultivated daffodils growing around the edges of the lawn and in the small woodland at the western edge of the garden which had been full of brambles when we arrived. In the summer of 2003 our friend Hughie had come with his chainsaw and cleared the ground under the trees and thinned out the more spindly ones allowing the daffodils to flourish. I really look forward to those weeks when the garden is full of their glowing yellow trumpets.

In 2007, the garden was especially beautiful because of Sue's efforts in clearing away the dead plants from the previous years, and I enjoyed walking amongst the daffodils when taking a break from my studies.

We had only seven of the original twenty-four cows left now and with the five remaining heifers that had come with them and our three Low Arvie heifers who had just had their first calf, this made sixteen altogether. They had produced only thirteen calves the previous autumn as the two oldest cows had been left to have a rest and Lady Freya had not had a calf either. These twenty-nine animals were all spending the winter, spring and early summer together in the Eastside field and so this had allowed us to keep the previous year's calves, who were now about eighteen months old, and we were hoping that we would be able to keep the seven steers until they were 'finished' and that the four heifers would fulfil their role as suckler cows in our herd to increase our now rather depleted numbers. When the six heifers from the newest batch reached maturity we would hopefully be back up to around twenty-four cows again and this was our goal. The new shed was planned to help us 'finish' all the progeny of these cows and all seemed to be going forward in a satisfactory manner towards this goal. In the meantime we thought we would be able to 'finish' the smaller numbers of steers so that they would live all their lives on Low Arvie and would be assured of the very best of care and attention to the end. Heinz and Yoghurt were now more than eighteen months old and were continuing to live out their days together in the old shed and the small paddocks. The plan was for Richard to take them together to the small abattoir in Lockerbie himself just before setting off on our Spanish trip. Here we were sure they would end their days in as calm and stress-free a manner as possible.

One day soon after the American ladies had left us, I was surprised to receive an email from Ron in Barry Smart's shop in Castle Douglas. He was the only person who had taken my books and sold them for me and by this time the sales had reached about four hundred. His email said that he had received a call from a television production company in North Yorkshire. This company produced a programme called 'The Dales Diary' and I had seen a few of the episodes on the television. Each week the programmes contained three presentations of ordinary but interesting people from around the Yorkshire Dales. The programme was presented by Luke Casey and took a gentle look at life in the country. The producers had rung Ron and explained that they were extending their area from Yorkshire to the Lake District, the Scottish Borders and Dumfries and Galloway and they were searching for likely subjects for their next series. He was asking me if I minded his telling them about us folks at Low Arvie and my book. I answered that I did not mind at all and in due course I received a telephone call from Barbara Buglass, who introduced herself as the producer of the programme. She asked if she could come and see us and asked me to send her a copy of 'The Ladies of Low Arvie'. I complied with her wishes and one Saturday in late April she arrived for coffee and cake and talked to us about their requirements for the programme. They had found five interesting people in Dumfries and Galloway and were to spend a week here filming the programmes in the middle of May. When I had told Richard of the initial call from Ron, he had not said much except that he hoped he wouldn't have to be involved, but when Barbara came, she quickly dismissed his reservations and said that he would certainly be a part of the 'piece'. Poor Richard had no choice in the matter, but as usual he met it with his usual stoicism and voiced no further objections.

Neither of us is very much given to seeking fame or glory, but, when I had reached my fiftieth birthday, I had taken stock of my life and discovered that I had not achieved very much and had not experienced much of excitement and I had vowed to try to change this. This explains my total acceptance of travelling to new places with Richard, of buying a farm and moving to Scotland, of publishing 'The Ladies' and of following my degree course with the OU. I now embraced the idea of a few minutes of fame on this television programme. I do, however, admit to a few bouts of nervousness as the day set for the filming, May 17th, approached!

Barbara had not really told us what to expect, only that they thought we would be fine for their purposes and that four people would be coming to spend the day with us. Once they arrived and introduced themselves, my nerves completely disappeared. There was a camera man, a sound man with one of those booms that you sometimes spot on outside broadcasts, Barbara and Luke.

They came into the house and had morning coffee whilst they discussed with us the format of the day. Luke refused to tell me any of the questions that he would ask us on camera as he said that this would detract from the spontaneity of our answers. I found this to be a little disturbing at first but he was such a charming man, so completely natural, and I soon felt as though I had known him for years, which made the forthcoming ordeals seem a little less daunting. There were to be shots of Richard and me walking round the farm discussing this and that, feeding the cows and walking amongst them. Then we would be taken off separately to be interviewed by Luke, before I was to read the introduction of 'The Ladies of Low Arvie' sitting in the kitchen.

We all went off into the new shed, which had not yet progressed further than the shell and the muddy floor area and we were filmed while Richard explained to me how the large area was to be divided up. Then I was taken off down the field and Luke asked me all kinds of questions about how we came to be at Low Arvie, what the house was like and all about the cows. He also asked about the differences I had found from my old life and this centred mainly on the water supply, which had caused us such problems in the early days. There was only a well that held a maximum of eighty gallons of water and I had found this to be very worrying, having only previously known the security of a mains supply. I explained that Richard had had to keep removing the heavy lid of the well several times a day so that I could see that the water was still there and I spoke of my relief when we finally had mains water piped across the mile of fields from the village. The end of the conversation centred on my writing of 'The Ladies,' which had brought the crew to us in the first place, and I spoke about how the book had come to be written. The only problem was that, as we are directly under the flight path of aeroplanes to America, the interview had to be interrupted several times whilst the drone of planes above us died away. When we had finished, Barbara said that it went well and she was happy with the way I had answered the questions.

Then it was Richard's turn and they all went off to the other side of the farm to do his interview. I was not allowed to be present and so I went back into the house to clear away the coffee things and begin preparing lunch. We had already invited the crew to have lunch at the farm instead of them having to go and find something to eat elsewhere and by the time they came back to the house, I had the table laden with ham rolls, salad and cakes. We spent a very pleasant hour chatting whilst we ate and we learnt that our section of the programme would take about eight minutes. This was a good chunk of the fifteen minutes of fame that we are all allowed, but still left us with seven more to come! (Still waiting!) Barbara couldn't, however, tell us when the programme would be shown, except that it would be sometime between September and Christmas. She thought that I may get requests for my book after the programme and so I asked that, if at all possible, we could be after the middle of October, when I would have done my three exams and my courses would be finished.

When lunch was over, we cleared the table and I was seated by the Aga to read the introduction. I had to do this three times, but they didn't explain why. When this was done, the cows were still grazing their way around the part of Eastside field nearest the house and Barbara said that they would like some shots of us feeding the cows. I went to the fence and called Beauty and she made her stately way up to the shed with the herd following her and we gave them a feed of straw. Richard and I were then filmed watching them and talking about them, whilst they behaved impeccably, munching away at the straw and taking no notice whatsoever of the four strangers and their equipment.

This was our part over and finished and after more tea and cake, the crew went off to film Luke arriving at the farm and talking about us to the audience. We then said goodbye and went back to the house to reflect upon our memories of the day and to revert to our normal life at the farm.

20

Study, Silage and Spain

I mentioned earlier the drawback with living out in the country, especially in Scotland, when trying to study with the OU. The fewer numbers of students and the wide distribution of the population mean that it is not always easy to get to the tutorials which are mainly held in Glasgow and Edinburgh. However, I found yet another advantage to having the apartment in Warwick, when I discovered that the OU tutorials in England are much more numerous and take place in many of the towns and cities. I searched the listings and found that all my courses had associated tutorials in and around the Midlands. I began to plan my visits down to Warwick to coincide with these and found myself travelling to Birmingham for Spanish classes, Nottingham for Latin and Oxford for Science. This made my life even busier as my time at home was spent keeping up to date with all the farm paperwork, trying to keep the house reasonably hygienic and filling the freezer and cake tins with enough provisions to keep Richard happy during my frequent absences. Along with attending the Spanish lessons on line and studying for all my three courses, life was quite hectic.

I was still studying on my train journeys and in spare minutes at the flat, as well as visiting Mother daily while in Warwick. She was very happy in Clarendon Manor but was gradually deteriorating physically, although her mental state had stabilised to a large extent. She didn't remember much about life in the outside world but was always pleased to see her family on our visits and we were always greeted with her beaming smile. The carers were obviously doing a good job of looking after her and I was able to concentrate on the other facets of my life without any concerns about her welfare. Catherine was also an excellent help to me at this time and was always happy to use some of her precious free time at weekends to spend time with her Grandmother at Clarendon Manor.

On the farm we had the three cows that had not got pregnant by the bull, Emerald, Jill and Gina all inseminated with Mochrum Kingfisher semen and these three were expected to calve in the early part of the next year. The other ten cows would all calve in the autumn and they were all fit and healthy and required only the usual care.

May and June passed by quickly in this way and I soon had to start thinking about preparing for our Spanish trip. We planned to leave on July 17th and drive down to Dover and cross the channel by ferry as this method of transport was cheaper than the Eurotunnel. Our first night would be spent at Gina's Bed and Breakfast establishment just south of Calais and renewing our acquaintanceship with her. From Gina's we would then drive in stages south through France to Spain and stay for two weeks in the apartment near Barcelona that we had first used in 1999. We spent most of the winters of 1999 and 2000 here and had become very friendly with Xavier and Merce who owned the apartment. The house had belonged to the owner of the vineyard which surrounded it and when Xavier had purchased the vineyard some years before, he had converted the house into three apartments. One of these was occupied by Josep and Meri-txell, a young couple who have also become lifelong friends. We were looking forward to spending time with them all again. After this sojourn, we would then drive across Northern Spain, stopping at hotels on the way and planned to arrive in Santiago del Compostela on August 4th for the start of the Spanish Summer School. At the end of the week, we would take a further week to drive home through western France.

I had two major concerns with these plans. The first was the silage. We were still in the Rural Stewardship Scheme whose rules decreed that we couldn't cut the grass for silage until after the first of July and we were anxious for the weather at the beginning of this month to be good enough to allow this to be done before we left. My second concern was also to do with the weather but for a completely different reason. I love living in Scotland for many reasons but not the least one is the fact that we do not get much very hot weather. I have never been a sun worshipper and in the few summers of my life that have been subject to sweltering heat, I have been found cowering behind closed curtains whilst most others luxuriated in the sunshine. I was worried that I would not be able to stand up to the summer heat of Northern Spain. However, there was nothing to be done about it, I had to participate in the Summer School in order to pass the course and so I tried to put my concerns to the back of my mind and got on with the preparations.

I was leaving the farm a few days before Richard to visit Mother and was staying on in Warwick on our return for the same reason. He was to drive down to Warwick on the 16th and we would leave for Dover early on the 17th.

As July approached I began to watch the weather forecast closely and was dismayed to see that there appeared to be no sign of any good weather on the horizon. We had met John and Suzie who were coming up to farm-sit and had felt relieved that they both exhibited qualities of common sense and confidence in their abilities to fulfil their role during our absence, so this caused us no worries. Also, we knew that Tom would see to the silage as soon as the weather allowed if it wasn't possible to do it before we left. He would cut and mow the grass and then arrange for it to be wrapped and baled in due course. This would leave the carting in to be done when we returned, although our friend Roy promised to call frequently to see that things were all well with John and Suzie and he said that he would make a start on the carting if he had time.

The cows were all fit and well and the grass was plentiful, so all that was necessary was to check on them for lameness or other health problems on a daily basis. On their preparatory visit to see the farm, John had said that he would be happy to see to Heinz and Yoghurt, moving them from one paddock to the other as they ate the grass down and giving them their daily ration and so we decided that they would not have to make their final journey as soon as July and could stay on the farm until they approached thirty months of age towards the end of the year. Regulations still in force after the BSE fiasco of the nineties means that British beef killed after the age of thirty months has to be treated in a different way, including the removal of the most dangerous parts of the carcase, and most farmers are still trying to finish their animals before this age. This is not difficult with the more commercial continental breeds and many are finished much sooner, but traditional breeds like Galloways and Highland cattle need all of this time.

Since there was nothing we could do about the weather and with all these plans in place for the farm, we continued to make our preparations for the journey.

21

Summer School

Iwas to be disappointed in my hopes for the weather, for July was a wet month in Scotland and very hot in Spain! There was no opportunity for Richard to do the silage before he left and so Tom was called upon to see to it for us. We knew that he was fully capable of doing this and would be well recompensed for his trouble and so we had no qualms about the situation, except our preference not to bother people and see to our affairs ourselves if at all possible.

John and Suzie's son and daughter-in-law arrived on schedule to take over the day before Richard was to leave and he was able to explain their minimal duties and wish them a good and restful two weeks. George is the organizer of the Lincoln Agricultural show which, for 2007, had taken place a few days before and so he was ready to put his feet up and relax after the stressful time that organizing such an event causes.

I spent three days visiting Mother before Richard arrived in Warwick and our holiday began. In spite of my hectic life, I had managed to keep up to date with all my OU assignments and was well on schedule with all the necessary work. I was thoroughly enjoying the Latin Course, as we were studying Virgil's Aeneid, concentrating on Book 2 of the 12 that make up the poem, and this was the one that I had studied for 'A' level back in 1965 so it was not entirely new to me. The Infectious Disease course was also proving fascinating and, although I was not gaining the high marks for this that I did in Latin assignments, I was doing well enough to be pleased with my progress. There was only one assignment left to do for this course, but this was a double weighted one and consisted of writing a scientific paper on one of three subjects. I had chosen to research the disease Cryptosporidiosis because the organism that causes it is carried in the guts of cattle and is spread by their effluent contaminating water sources. The organism is not killed by the chlorine which is used to disinfect our drinking water and if it contaminates water supplies and swimming pools it can lead to serious outbreaks of disease and is difficult to control. It is also prevalent in areas that do not have mains water, as Low Arvie was when we arrived there, and, with the proximity of grazing animals to private water supplies, such as mountain streams and unprotected wells, these regions have to be well monitored. Doctors in these areas have to maintain vigilance and, as I discovered during my research for the project, there is a stringent reporting system in place. I had visited the Scottish Agricultural Colleges laboratories in Dumfries and those of the Scottish Water Board near Edinburgh and saw at first hand the testing systems for this and the other 'nasties' that find their way into our water that occur behind the scenes on a daily basis. I then had spoken to the director of the Public Health Board in Dumfries and he had given me a breakdown of his role in the process. I received the statistics for the number of outbreaks of this disease in Dumfries and Galloway over the previous ten years and I was hopeful of putting together a good report of my findings. My challenge would be to keep it within the 1500 word allowance, as I had so much interesting and relevant information to collate. I spent my time in Warwick before Richard's arrival in sorting through this information and planning the rough outline of my writing up and then I put it to one side to be finished on our return from Spain.

I was not so confident about my work for the Spanish course, in spite of the 'extra' year I had given to it through studying with Jan. I had passed 'O' level Spanish back in 1965 but then had had no further contact with the language until our visit in 1999. On our arrival for that first visit, my Spanish consisted of a primeval memory of a few words. Richard had spent two years back in the 1970s in Ecuador helping the native population to find better ways to store potatoes, protecting them from the heat rather than the cold as we have to here. At that time he had been a fluent Spanish speaker and the remnants of the language that remained in his memory were better than mine and I had relied heavily on him to translate for me in the first days of our stay. Xavier's first language is Catalan and so we had had some very funny conversations. However, we must have communicated well enough because our planned week's stay had lengthened into six and by the end of the first fortnight we had been adopted as 'family'. Josep and Meri-txell also became regular visitors to our apartment to drink tea and chat, and, although both spoke reasonable English, they steadfastly refused to do so and so my Spanish had improved considerably over the weeks. Our return trip in 2000 had lasted for ten weeks and the improvement had continued. I had thought that this would stand me in good stead when starting out on the OU Spanish courses four years later, but I soon became disillusioned about this, because my Spanish, which served very well as a communicating tool with good friends over a pot of tea, was full of mistakes that were not appreciated by the OU tutors and I found it very difficult to 'unlearn' them and replace them with the correct format. Jan had started learning her Spanish with the first OU course and had therefore learnt correctly from the beginning. She was a good partner for me as, being a trained teacher as well, she had helped me to correct many of these misconceptions during our years of study together and by now I was at least on the right track, if not gaining the high marks that she had.

The journey down to Barcelona through France was uneventful and pleasant. We enjoyed renewing our acquaintance with Gina and catching up on her news. Then we made our way quite slowly southwards, stopping off at some charming Chambres d'hote along the way. Our preferred method of travel is to cover no more than two hundred miles a day, setting off after a leisurely breakfast and following a route that does not include motorway travel, stopping for coffee and lunch in wayside cafes and tabacs. Apart from the week in Edinburgh, this was Richard's first holiday since going to the farm in 2002 and we were determined to make it a good one. We would be away from the farm for five weeks altogether and we both felt that this was a bonus that we could not have contemplated when moving to Scotland.

The weather in Spain was very hot and we were not inclined to do much more than enjoy the company of Xavier's family and that of Josep and Meri-txell during our two weeks at the apartment. Richard likes the sun and heat and spent his spare time sitting under the shade of the trees in the garden reading and I hovered indoors with the windows wide open and the sun shades down. Fortunately there was a breeze that wafted in from time to time and kept things reasonably comfortable for me. We spent the hottest day of our stay, when the temperature reached 37 degrees Centigrade visiting El Priorat, a National Park where there are lots of beautiful Spanish villages and the countryside is covered with vineyards, with Josep and Meri-txell. We drove slowly taking in the beauty of the scenery from one village to the next and found that each had a central plaza or square where there were the most beautiful trees all in bloom at that time, and which gave plenty of shade under which to sit and cool off with iced tea and lemonade. Just as we were beginning to droop with the heat, we would get back into Josep's air conditioned car and drive on. As well as the villages we visited, we called at several vineyards and bought wine and olive oil to bring home and it was a lovely day of which we retain very happy memories.

All too soon it was time to take our leave of our friends and set off for Santiago. Cities and towns are not our most favourite places and certainly the beauty of the architecture in Santiago was spoilt for me by the stifling heat and the thousands of pilgrims who were visiting the shrine of Saint James in the cathedral. Legend has it that James was one of the apostles who went to Spain to preach after the death of Christ. He returned to Palestine, but was captured and tortured to death in AD 44 by Herodes Agrippa, who refused to allow the body to be buried. In the night James' body was taken by his disciples and brought to Northern Spain by boat where he was buried secretly. Eight hundred years later a burial place was found in woods on the Campus Stellae (hence Compostela) and a chapel was built in which the body was placed. The town of Santiago grew up around the chapel and pilgrims began to visit. This pilgrimage grew and the Way of Saint James (Camino de Santiago) is travelled today by 100 000 people each year. They come by all and any means and the roads around the town abound with paths and signposts bearing the cockle shell emblem of Saint James and which lead to the shrine containing the relics in the huge cathedral at the centre of this World Heritage town.

This great influx of people meant that walking down the narrow streets of the old part of the city was reduced to a shuffle, and the heat, combined with the proximity of so many bodies, did not make it a very pleasurable process, to say the least! At each shop doorway, we were accosted by girls in national costume begging us to try Spanish delicacies which they held out on large platters to try and tempt us into their shop to buy more.

I think you may gather that my memories of Santiago are not terribly exhilarating and confirmed my long held feelings that the countryside is my preferred environment!

I cannot say that the Summer School was very edifying either. There was no grouping by ability and I found myself in a class which contained several housewives who had rich husbands with boats moored around Spain, who were just there to try and pick up the odd word or two of Spanish in order to give instructions to their maids. They had no real grasp of the language and didn't take the work seriously, but giggled and chatted their way through. The tutor obviously had no teacher training and his delivery was dull and boring. The only really good thing that I found about the process was in meeting up with my 'internet' friends face to face. We had all arranged to go on the same week and it was nice to see the people who had only been voices before. Even Jan had travelled to Santiago to join us in our leisure time, though she had now progressed onto the level 3 course, and it was wonderful to see them all.

The other benefit of being in a University building was that there was access to the Internet, and I was able to send and receive emails to and from John and Suzie. They had taken over the care of the farm from George and his wife and were able to tell us that the weather had finally allowed Tom to start the silage on August 4th. By the 7th it was all finished AND Roy had made a start with the carting. This was a big relief to us and we left Santiago to begin the journey home on the 11th with happier minds.

22

Accident!

When we had got the Ladies settled into Low Arvie back in 2002, we had turned our attention to equipping ourselves with the necessary transport required to take such large animals from place to place. Once again we were subject to EU rules and regulations and set about searching for the correct transporter to do this. We were intending to buy a livestock trailer at one of the farm sales we attended in those early days, but before we could do this we had to find a suitable vehicle with which to pull it. We both had our own cars, Richard's being a Ford Scorpio and mine a small green Hyundai Atoz, neither of which was fit for the purpose and so we began to search the advertisements for a suitable vehicle. One morning after Christmas Richard suggested that we should drive to the Landrover garage in Carlisle and 'interview' a Landrover Freelander which they had for sale.

We went out in this car with the salesman to put it through its paces around the countryside obstacle course that they used to demonstrate the handling properties of their vehicles. The car performed reasonably well up and down the obstacles and through the muddy areas of the course, but neither of us was totally convinced that it was the vehicle for us. On returning to the garage showroom, we moved on to looking at a Landrover Discovery that was for sale. I got into the passenger seat and thought that it felt more substantial for the farm work that it was to do, but when Richard sat in the driving seat, he found that his knees were very close to the dashboard beneath the steering wheel and therefore it did not afford him a very comfortable driving position. We were quite disappointed at this point, as the need to find a suitable vehicle had become quite urgent as we had had the Ladies now for several months and we were anxious to equip ourselves with the facility to transport them. We had decided to trade in both our cars and buy a multipurpose vehicle which would serve for both farm work and private use and, as we only intended to have the one vehicle, it needed to be comfortable enough for any personal journeys that we might make too. On the far side of the showroom stood a gleaming new dark blue Range Rover with a £60 000 price ticket across the windscreen. Whilst Richard spoke to the salesman, I wandered over to it and opened the door. It was beautiful, with soft leather seats and all manner of knobs and screens arrayed along its dashboard. I got in and immediately fell in love with it! It was comfortable in the extreme and I could understand its high price when I studied all of the equipment it contained. Jokingly I shouted to Richard, 'This is the one we want.' He came over and looked at the vehicle and then at the price ticket and said, 'If only!' We left the car and went back to take our leave of the salesman. I expressed my admiration of the Range Rover and said I wished we could afford that one. 'Well,' he said, 'we have a second hand one on the forecourt at a reasonable price. Would you like to try it out?' I looked to where he was pointing and saw the most beautiful pale gold version standing in the line of Discoveries and Freelanders. It was the top of the range model with every bolt on goody that it was possible to have. It was just two years old with 22000 miles on the clock, but the price was reasonable for two reasons. It was a vehicle that had been imported from Spain, even though it was a right hand drive, and this apparently negated part of the warranty on it, and it was a petrol model instead of the more usual diesel. The first drawback didn't seem too important to us but we had wanted a diesel vehicle as Richard had bought a new diesel tank so that we could purchase diesel in bulk at a cheaper price than buying it at a garage. Furthermore diesel engines apparently are more economical and last longer than petrol ones.

I was quite surprised, therefore, when Richard agreed to take the vehicle out for a test drive, but I quickly went outside and got in it before he could change his mind. The dark blue model in the showroom paled into insignificance beside this beautiful golden version and I was smitten. However, I still didn't think that we would buy it as it was dearer than the other vehicles we had looked at and it didn't fulfil the diesel criterion, but I was planning to enjoy the test drive – and I did! Happily it fulfilled my criteria for buying a car, which are different to Richard's. I had been driving cars with automatic gearboxes for several years and I now felt that this was number one on my list. I also wanted comfort in both driving and passenger positions and lots of little storage places and cup holders for picnics, and also plenty of airbags to make me feel safe. The car was superb and I was even brave enough to take the driving seat for a few miles.

Richard said very little, whilst I enthused audibly and lengthily about its lovely leather seats, the leather casing on the steering wheel and the integrated Satnav with its little screen in the middle of the dashboard. Whilst Richard was driving, I investigated all the little cubby holes and demonstrated to him the fancy arrangement of cup holders that I found.

Imagine my surprise when we returned to the garage and Richard began to ask the salesman about the trade-in values of our two cars. I was shocked into silence (very rare) and held my breath until I heard him say that we would buy the vehicle!

I have been driving since 1971 and have owned a car of my own ever since. I hope I am not tempting providence by saying that, although I have had many scrapes in that time, I have never hit either a person or a moving vehicle. I lost the sight in my right eye in an early childhood accident with a bow and arrow, which means that I have no binocular vision and my manoeuvring in tight spaces has never been of advanced driving standard, a fact which causes my son-in-law much amusement when I am attempting to reverse park the little Suzuki that I keep in Warwick in front of their house. Through the years I have had contretemps with trees, houses, walls, telegraph poles, gates, lamp posts and even the other family car which was parked next to mine on the drive. I knocked seven corners off one car I had and in the end gave up having them repaired, but I repeat, I have never hit a person or a moving vehicle. For this reason buying such a large vehicle as the Range Rover was quite scary. It was so beautiful, that I would have been devastated to spoil its gleaming golden paintwork, but I found that sitting up so high enabled me to see where I was on the road better than in a lower car and made manoeuvring easier and, surprisingly, all the corners stayed intact!

When we went to Spain, we had had the car for four and a half years and it had never given us any trouble in all that time. We hoped that it would last us for at least six more years and by that time we may not even need another powerful vehicle as we may have come to the end of our farming life. The seats were so comfortable on the long journey to Barcelona and onwards to Santiago that it was like sitting in an armchair. We even managed to up the petrol consumption by 25% by driving so sedately.

On our return, Richard dropped me in Warwick and then went back to Low Arvie, while I caught up with Mother and Catherine for several days. I then caught the train back to Dumfries, where Richard picked me up.

He had spent the intervening days working towards getting the shed finished and wanted to call and see the plumber who was going to install the pipe work and water troughs and so we made a detour off the A75 onto the country lane where the plumber had his headquarters. Having completed the business about the troughs, we got back in the car and set off home. We were discussing the information we had just gained from the plumber as we drove out of his drive and I was surprised to watch Richard steer the car carefully onto the right hand side of the road. I don't think I had time to say anything, when, just as he had straightened the wheel on the right hand carriageway, a small white van came steaming round the bend in front of us at a high rate of knots. I looked at Richard in horror and could see the consternation on his face. 'What is this van doing on the wrong side of the road?' was the thought that was plainly going through his head. This was the first time he had driven the car with me in it since driving 4000 miles on the continent and, with his attention on our conversation, his brain had obviously reverted to this former pattern of driving. There was only time for him to attempt to move over as close as possible to the right hand verge, hoping that the van driver would get onto what Richard thought was his proper side (which he obviously didn't) before the van hit us head on. Or almost head on, because our car was now pointing right and the van hit the front left hand corner of our car in front of me. The tank like qualities of the Range Rover meant that Richard was uninjured, and I only had a bruised knee and a sore chest from the tightening of the seat belt, although obviously we were both badly shaken. The airbags remained in place. The van suffered much worse damage and its driver was obviously injured.

Thankfully, my brain remained quite active and I undid my seatbelt and quickly found my mobile phone and dialled 999. Richard got out and went to see what he could do for the van driver.

Within a very short time, a paramedic on a motorbike was arriving and he took over seeing to the injured man. He got him out of the van, from which smoke had begun to appear and he shouted at us to move away from the vehicles. I ran up the road, I suppose because I could think of nothing else to do, and was dismayed to see a fire engine passing by on the A75. He had obviously missed the turning for the lane and in the precious minutes that he took to turn round and come back, the smoke from the van's engines had become mixed with flames. In a blur, a police car arrived and an ambulance came and took the injured man away. The police woman took Richard off into her car and I was left to my own confused devices to watch the firemen finish dousing the flames which had consumed all the engine compartment of the burning van. By this time other vehicles were queuing down the road and by chance the first one in the queue was the plumber's workman who was returning to the yard. I went and spoke to him and he said that he would come back and take us home as it looked as if our car was undriveable.

The police woman came and asked me for my account and all I could say, as Richard had, was that we were on the wrong side of the road and explain the reason. It didn't make it any less Richard's fault but it was a genuine reason.

In a while a recovery truck appeared and the driver winched my beautiful golden Range Rover onto the back and drove it away.

Sadly I never saw it again.

23

Aftermath

Our first concern after the accident was for the van driver and the next day Richard rang the police in Dumfries to find out what had happened to him. To our great relief we learned that the man had been treated for two broken ribs and then allowed to leave hospital. They promised to let us know any further information about the man, but the fact that we never received any allowed us to think that he had recovered in time.

Next we had to go through the process of finding out about the Range Rover. The insurance company dealt with all the necessary processes for this and we were very sad when we received their letter telling us that the cost of repairs to such an expensive vehicle made it uneconomic to repair and they were writing it off. With the demise of the old van some time before, this left us without a farm vehicle of any kind, and without a vehicle that I could drive. Fortunately Richard did have another car available to him. He owns an old Saab 9000 Turbo, which is his pride and joy, although it had been wrapped in old sheets in various garages since 1996. It had required some work to be done on it to get it roadworthy, including the fitting of a new exhaust pipe, which had been purchased in 2003 and had spent the next four years lying beside the car on the workshop floor! In June Roy had begun coming to Low Arvie two days a week to help Richard make a start on getting the new shed finished and, when work on the shed was held up or the weather was too bad to be outside, they had worked together on the Saab and it was now almost back to driveable condition. They finished off the remaining jobs and Richard took the Saab to get an MOT certificate and make us mobile again.

It was two months before the claim on the Range Rover was finally sorted out and we could start to look for a more suitable vehicle for the farm work. I was convinced that we would not be able to afford to replace it with a vehicle of similar quality and beauty as the golden Range Rover, and I felt glad that I had had the pleasure of owning it for four years but very sad at its demise and we began to think that we would try and find one of the newer models of Discovery that had come to the market some time before and which had better leg room for Richard At this time, our farmer friend, Graham, had decided to buy a Landrover Defender for his farm and, during one of our shared Sunday lunches at Pringles bar, he had asked Richard to go with him to look at them. One of the farmers in the area had diversified into dealing in these farm vehicles and Graham thought that, as well as Defenders, he would have some Discoveries for sale too. This man travelled down to England on a regular basis and purchased vehicles at one of the auctions near Hereford. These were vehicles that had been owned by the richer inhabitants of the south and then traded in for an upgrade after one or two years. I decided to go along with them to ensure that any likely vehicle that Richard might be tempted to buy had the correct conformation of cubby holes and cup holders!

Imagine my delight, therefore, when we arrived at the farm, to see, standing amid the line of Defenders and Discoveries, a shiny dark green three-year-old Range Rover. Apparently the farmer's wife occasionally had to make long journeys around Scotland and he purchased a comfortable vehicle at the auction for this purpose. Once the journey was over, he sold the vehicle and repeated the exercise the next time that she needed to travel again.

I did pay lip service to the three Discoveries that were on offer and investigated their cubby holes but it was no contest! The Range Rover wasn't quite top of the range, but it was automatic AND powered by diesel, and, although it had no Satnav, there were sufficient cup holders and cubby holes. Furthermore it was two years newer than the now defunct golden car and had only had one previous owner who had covered less than 20000 miles in it. Even more important for Richard's bank balance, it was just as reasonably priced as the previous one had been. We agreed there and then to buy it and, joy oh joy, the seller said that it could be ready for the road by the Wednesday. I would be mobile again!

The only remaining cloud on the horizon was the wait to see what action the police would take against Richard over the accident. We philosophized to each other that the accident had happened and couldn't be undone, it was clearly Richard's fault and so whatever happened as a result would have to be borne with a good grace. Every day I expected Brian the postman to bring bad tidings, but time went on and we heard nothing. We got the Range Rover and life reverted back to normality and still no letter came from the police. Was it possible, we began to wonder, that the powers that be had accepted our explanation? We knew that the van had been travelling at high speed on the country lane and wondered if this made a difference to the case. Also we thought that the driver had not been wearing his seat belt, which had contributed to his injuries. Our car had been stationary when the collision occurred, a fact that was proved because our airbags had not opened. All these things could have been taken into consideration. For twelve months I worried about what would happen, but when, after this time we had still heard nothing, we began to hope that this would remain the case. It has!

However, the accident did seem to be the start of a run of bad fortune that dogged us in the following months.

24

More Trials

Our ill luck continued when the Klondyke bull, Livewire, whom we had hired from Scott in November went lame after only one week with us, but Scott had replaced him with Blackcraig Gusto, who was the father of the three Klondyke bulls that had been to Low Arvie. Like Zeppelin, he was a gentle giant and showed no aggression whatsoever, even when coming to feed. The three younger bulls had all pushed their way through the cows and calves to get to the feed barrier first and, having eaten their portion, had then bullied the cows away from theirs. But Gusto was a true gentleman and allowed the cows their full share. Unlike his young sons who were not yet fully grown, his head was massive and there was only one space in the feed barrier that was big enough for him. At first he would try the smaller spaces and, not being able to reach the food, he would walk away and cry like a baby, but hunger and our encouragement soon trained him to find the correct one and he would then stand quietly munching away at the pile of feed that we gave him. There were seventeen Ladies all vying for his attention, thirteen 'old hands' and the four 'first time' heifers born in 2005. The three other cows that were inseminated back in May and June were all in calf and would not be requiring his services. This meant that the number of animals on the farm had crept back up to 52 and included the ten young calves, thirteen yearlings and nine two year old steers including Heinz and Yoghurt.

The shed was nearing completion, thanks to some hard work on Richard's part and a lot of help from Roy and we should now be able to fulfil the plan of keeping all our stock to finishing as we had planned.

Throughout the aftermath of the accident, I still had to finish off my Cryptosporidiosis assignment and prepare for the three exams that were on my agenda for October. On my visits to Warwick, I worked hard at the assignment and was very pleased with the finished result. I was even more delighted when I received my tutor's feedback to discover that she, too, had thought it good enough to award me 100% for it. This result raised my overall assignment marks above the 85% distinction level and put pressure on me to try and match this mark in the exam. I was hopeful of gaining this figure in the Latin exam and if I could achieve a Distinction in the Infectious Disease course too, I would have fulfilled a major criterion for an overall First Class Honours degree. I would just need to achieve a reasonable pass in the remaining 60 points worth of courses the next year.

The accident was an unwelcome background to my exam preparations but, at the time, it did not seem to affect my studying and it is only whilst I have been writing about it that I am realising that it must have been quite a difficult time for me. However, I do not offer it as any kind of excuse.

When the exam results appeared on my OU website page I was really disappointed. I had achieved only 84% in the Latin exam, 79% in the Infectious Disease one and 69% for the Spanish one. This gave me Grade 2s in the first two which required 85% for Distinction and Grade 3 in Spanish which required 70% for Grade 2. I was not surprised or disappointed about the Infectious Disease result but missing higher grades by just 1% in Spanish and especially in Latin had a devastating effect on me and brought on a return of the depression that I had suffered throughout my earlier life. I tried to rationalise that achieving two Grade 2s and a Grade 3 in such high level exams would delight many people but I could not agree for myself. I had been so pleased with the work that I had done throughout the year and the 1% deficit in the two exams was very hard to take. A 10% deficit would have been much easier to come to terms with. It also meant that my dream of a First Class Honours degree was all but over. I would need to achieve Distinctions in the three Science courses for which I had registered for the forthcoming year, and in my heart of hearts I knew that this would not be possible. I had been banking on the Grade 1 for Latin and missing it by so little was a big blow that even finding and buying the new Range Rover could not assuage.

Neither could the showing of our Dales Diary programme in early December. The programme was shown in Yorkshire at the end of November and in Dumfries and Galloway the next week. It was not a very pleasurable experience watching myself on television but Richard, the farm and the Ladies all looked beautiful. The editors had done a good job of making a piece of television that flowed and told our story effectively and well.

In the following weeks, I received many requests for copies of 'The Ladies' and when I checked the iUniverse website I saw that their sales had also increased by more than two hundred. Even this welcome news did not really help to lift my depression, although it raised my book sales to just under 650, only fifty short of the magic 700 figure that I had read one had to achieve to be called a 'real' author. It was many more than I had ever dreamed of and with commercial sales only being made in Barry Smart's book shop and no marketing except the television programme, I was happy with the result.

To make my life even more difficult at this time, I was trying to give what support I could to my brother, whose wife had left him in the summer. He was also in deep depression and I was speaking to him on a daily basis, listening to the long list of regrets he had about the way his life had turned out. I was spending Christmas at Low Arvie that year and joining Catherine and Morgan for New Year, and I felt that the least we could do was to invite Philip to spend the festive season away from his now lonely environment and join Richard and me. It was therefore a fairly sombre affair.

I was in the middle of cooking Christmas lunch when the telephone rang and, on lifting the receiver, I heard Catherine sobbing. In between the sobs, she told me that she had gone to Clarendon Manor to find that Mother had had what appeared to be a stroke and that she was unconscious. My immediate thought was to get in the car and drive the three hundred miles that separated us, but this was not very practical as it would have taken me at least six hours and Catherine needed some support immediately. My practical mind must have kicked in through the levels of my depression and I began to think around the problem. There were no trains down to Leamington either

Christmas Day or Boxing Day and I already had my tickets for my planned journey down there on the 27th so there seemed little point in changing this plan if I could help Catherine in some other way. Morgan was on duty at the fire station and my mind searched around for other sources of help.

Philip's first wife, who is also Catherine's godmother, lives just four miles from Leamington and she has always remained a part of our family in spite of the breakdown of the marriage many years before. She knew Catherine well and, I knew she would help if she could. I told Catherine to stay where she was and that I would call her back as soon as possible. I then prayed that Joan and her partner Norman had not gone away for Christmas.

Quickly I dialled her number and explained our dilemma. Her response was immediate and her Christmas dinner preparations were handed over to Norman, while she put on her coat and went to Catherine's aid. She phoned a little later to say that Catherine was calmer after the shock she had received and that Mother had regained consciousness and seemed to be responding well. The Carers complied with our request to keep Mother at Clarendon Manor and let Nature take its course one way or the other and when Catherine visited her later in the day, she was able to report that Mother seemed to be recovering well.

By the time I arrived in Leamington two days later, she was once more getting up and following her usual daily routine and the crisis passed.

By then Norman had gone off down south somewhere to officiate at a New Year's firework display and so Joan joined Philip and me at Catherine's for a reasonably happy New Year's Eve celebration and Richard enjoyed Hogmanay in the peace and quiet of Galloway with the Ladies.

25

Calamity!

The sadness that was surrounding our lives at this time continued when, on January 8th 2008, Richard took Heinz and Yoghurt on their final journey to Lockerbie. Yoghurt was fast approaching thirty months of age and so we said goodbye in the knowledge that we had seen them through a life of contentment and good care right to the end. In many ways it was a relief not to have to watch over Heinz anymore, making sure he didn't bump into things and that he always found his way to his food. He usually managed to stay close to Yoghurt when they were moving between the paddocks, and he did come to respond to Richard's directions to veer left or right when he was getting too near to the house or shed wall, but there were still some distressing times.

Also we had managed to finish the remaining seven steers from the same age group and we felt quite lucky to have passed the assessment to send them to be sold in the Wholefoods supermarkets in London. This company source their food from the producers and only sell what they can assure their customers is produce reared or grown in a wholesome way. They paid a small premium for this and we had received a visit in the early summer from one of their representatives to view our farm and the methods we use to rear our cattle. Their buyer, Billy Grazebrook, had come and viewed our steers and declared that they were ready to go and the date for their collection was fixed for January 21st.

On the 20th there was a happier occurrence which served to lift my mood a little, when I received a telephone call from friends that I had lost touch with ten years before. By chance, they had seen us on 'The Dales Diary' and had tracked me down through buying my book and then searching the Internet. They seemed to be as delighted as I was to re-make contact and we agreed to meet up again as soon as was possible.

However, I was still very down when the books for the new courses I had registered for arrived and, after opening and reading the remit for the first course on the list, I was not too happy with it. Following the success of my Cryptosporidiosis report, I had chosen to finish the final year of my studying by doing the 30 point Science in Society project course, wondering if I could repeat the success. I had also booked to do two 15 point practical courses to be held at Nottingham University in July and August of 2008. These made up the full complement of my Honours degree. I also had to do a level 2 course alongside the project course as this should really have been done first. On opening the parcel, I discovered that the project was not the same type as the Crypto one, with only 50% of it made up with scientific research and the remaining half needing to be related to ethical considerations. As my interest in the Crypto report had been captured by the scientific research that I was learning to do, the thought of having to match this with research that was more social science in aspect was not very appealing. I was still disillusioned with my performance in the exams and, now that I had gained enough points for an ordinary BSc, I discussed with Richard calling it a day and cancelling the studies for that year. He said that it would be a shame not to finish what I had set out to do and, given my predilection for quitting, I decided that he was quite right and so I set out my stall once more to begin my studies.

The lorry to fetch the steers was to come very early on the 21st and, as I am no use whatsoever at loading times and do not like to be involved in watching the cattle leave the farm, I stayed in bed whilst Richard got up and dressed at 6a.m. I heard the lorry drive into the yard soon after Richard's departure and I switched on the radio to drown out the noise of the engine. Writing this makes me feel very cowardly at leaving this unpleasant part of the process entirely to Richard but I am much more emotional than he is and struggle to come to terms with it. I know it is the whole purpose of our business but I am much happier dealing with the cows and calves in their early days and making the lives of the animals as good as it can be. I knew that the loading process should not take long and I huddled down under the covers to wait for the lorry to leave.

This was quite an important day for the business as it was the culmination of the process we had set out to achieve almost five years before: to see our own reared beef finished on the farm. All being well, with the land in some sort of shape, the new shed operational and the suckler herd almost back to full strength, we now had the business that we wanted.

I waited for the lorry to leave, but I could still hear the drone of its engine above the radio, when I heard another vehicle come up the drive and into the yard. My mind only registered this fact and did not question why a second vehicle had come at such an early hour and in a little while I heard the lorry rev up and drive away. I was just about to jump out of bed and put the kettle on to make Richard a warming cup of tea after his early morning work in the darkness of a cold January morning, when I was startled to hear a shout from below. 'Hello', cried the strange voice, 'Are you there? A man's been kicked!' I pushed my arms into my dressing gown and ran downstairs to find a very pale looking Richard seated on the stool by the back door with one leg sticking out at a strange angle and a man I recognised as Derek Thompson, the lorry owner, attempting to help him up. My fuddled brain couldn't take the scene in and it took a minute for Derek's explanation to sink in. One of the steers had kicked out and Richard had been standing in just the wrong place and had received the full force of the animal's hoof on his knee. Our animals rarely kick and he had been completely unprepared for such a happening. The knock had sent him sick and all he had been able to do was hobble to the side of the shed and hang over the feed barrier. He had been unable to take any further part in the loading and the lorry driver had had to phone Derek to come and help. This explained the arrival of the second vehicle. The two men had finished the loading whilst Richard remained transfixed by the pain and then Derek had stayed behind and helped Richard into the house.

Unbelievably now, I was not worried by this occurrence, only concerned to get Richard some attention. He is very fit and has suffered many knocks and blows in his life, which he has always shrugged off with no fuss and I must have assumed that this would be the same. His colour was returning a little now and he hobbled his way into the kitchen, whilst I found a bag of frozen peas to place on his knee and we assessed the situation. He was obviously in great pain and the three of us decided that the best thing to do would be to call for medical help and so I dialled 999 to request an ambulance and paramedics. Derek stayed for a little while, but assured that help was on its way, he left to get on with his day's work

When they arrived some twenty minutes later, Richard was looking a lot better and the paramedics, who were right at the end of their fourteen hour shift, diagnosed bad bruising and suggested rest as the answer, but they would, they said, take Richard to Dumfries Infirmary if he felt it was necessary. My concern only grew a little, when Richard said that he wanted to do this and it was soon agreed that he should go with them in the ambulance and I would follow in the car when I had got dressed, to bring him home after his treatment. The ambulance man said, 'You'll manage to walk alright to the ambulance, will you?' and, not wanting to create a fuss, Richard stood on his good leg and proceeded to attempt this feat. It was plain that this was a massive challenge and that his right leg would not bear his weight, but somehow he managed to shuffle his way through the door and into the vehicle.

When they had left, I rang Roy and asked if he could come and see to feeding the cattle that morning. He had been helping Richard with the completion of the new shed since the summer and had often helped him with the cattle, so they were used to him and he knew their routine. He said he would come straightaway and then come back later in the afternoon to feed if Richard was still incapacitated and to see what the diagnosis was.

It must have been the shock that kept my mind from pondering anything other than the minor inconvenience that I felt we would suffer from the incident. I fully expected to arrive at the hospital to find Richard bandaged up, maybe with a packet of painkillers in his hand, ready to come back home.

The reality, however, was very different. He was in one of the cubicles in the A&E department, lying on the bed with his knee immobilised, but he was quite cheerful. He had already been wheeled to the X-ray department and was now waiting for the result. Nurses appeared from time to time to offer him painkillers and ask various questions and one of these told us that the X-ray was back and they were waiting for the doctor to come and evaluate it. They were all appearing to imply that the injury might be more serious than we had thought and slowly alarm bells began to start tuning up in the back of my mind. No bandages were appearing and there was no talk of going home.

In a short time, a young man appeared in the cubicle. He introduced himself as the doctor and proceeded to tell us his assessment of the X-ray. The kick had impacted right by the side of Richard's knee cap and there was a clear vertical break at the top of the tibia bone. The X-ray was displayed on the computer in the nurses' station and he took me to see what he was talking about. I could clearly see the fracture. The top of the tibia bone splays out into a flat triangle and the femur, or thigh bone, sits on the top of this triangle and makes the knee joint. A triangular corner of the top of the tibia had received the full force of the animal's kick and had broken away. The broken portion was roughly one and a half centimetres along each of its three sides and was at a drunken angle to the rest. We went back to Richard and the doctor continued to tell us the implications. He required a complicated operation in which a metal plate would be inserted along the edge of the tibia and then screws would be fixed through the plate and through the broken piece of bone to join it back into place. The leg would then be splinted and Richard would have to keep any weight off it for four or five months while the bone healed. He would be in hospital for about ten days and then on crutches for the four or five months of the healing process.

I finally felt the full horror of the situation and the alarm bells were suddenly playing very loud tunes. This was January 21st. We had 43 animals that required feeding on a daily basis until at least May and, whilst I could manage to give them their daily cake ration, there was no way I could fetch in the feed trailers and put in the fresh silage bales that they required. The bales weigh about half a tonne and have to be lifted up on the spikes of the Matbro handler and then the plastic jackets and the confining net wrapping underneath removed before they are dropped in the feed trailer. Then the trailer has to be pulled by the tractor to its position in the field. With the best will in the world, I was totally incapable of doing this. I could see no way in which we could continue the farm. How ironic that the very day we had achieved the goal of our business should turn out to be its last!

When the doctor left us to arrange Richard's admission, we looked at each other and I could feel the tears welling up in my eyes. For once there were no words to express our feelings. Richard could do or say nothing that would help as he could see no way forward for the farm either. I just had to assure him that I would see to the sale of the cattle and beg him to concentrate on getting his leg better and we consoled ourselves that, at least, we had had five years of his dream and had proved our ability to create and run a successful venture.

I left him waiting for admission to the main hospital and said I would return later in the day and tell him what I had done. Once outside the hospital, the full range of my emotions kicked in and I stood by the hospital wall as my tears flowed. I took out my mobile phone and rang the one person who would understand what I was feeling – Catherine. I told her what had happened and that I was going home to sell the cows. Begging me to be careful driving home in such a state, she promised to ring me back as soon as she could. She was going to try and get the rest of that day and the next off work and come up to Scotland immediately.

When my tears slowed, I got back in the car and drove slowly home.

26

David, Henry and other friends

I have not previously mentioned the other two important members of Low Arvie farm staff and this seems as good a time as any to do so. When we first got the cows in 2002 and started to store their food, we decided that it would be a good idea to find some rodent operatives to patrol the sheds and keep the mice and rats away. When we returned Zeppelin the bull after his visit to create our first batch of calves to his owner, Gordon Gilligan, at his home at High Creoch farm near Gatehouse of Fleet, Gordon mentioned that they had just had two litters of kittens and were looking for homes for some of them. There were three that were not ordered and so we said that we would take them when they were ready to leave their mother. In the following weeks, someone else asked Gordon if they could have the female kitten, and when he rang to see what we thought, we agreed that we had really only wanted two and were happy just to have the two males.

Richard stressed to me that they would not be 'real' pets, but would be expected to live in the barn and patrol the farm to fulfil their important function of keeping the feed and environment free from rodent contamination. Rats had been my worst worry when coming to the farm, as, like most people, I hate them, and so I was pleased that we were taking this step to help protect our area. In all the years, I have only ever seen one rat on the farm and Richard has found a handful of dead ones and so I feel that the steps he takes to keep the feed areas clean and the presence of the cats is a very successful policy.

We fetched the cats when they were just five and six weeks old, obviously they were from different litters and one was jet black with large blue eyes and the other was ginger. Richard had fenced off one corner of the barn and we had put in Mother's old wicker clothes baskets with a blanket, a pile of straw, which they had been used to, being born in Gordon's barn, some food and a drink and Richard had also made a 'hidey hole' by leaning a piece of wood against the wall. The kittens were so tiny that they did not even make a handful and when we put them into their new home, they both made straight for the 'hidey hole' behind the wood. It was almost bedtime and so we left them there and hoped they would be alright.

The next morning the kittens were still huddled together behind the wood and the food and drink were untouched. We brought them into the kitchen and I warmed some milk and found two eye droppers from the medicine cabinet. Richard took the black one and I held the ginger one while we offered them the milk. They both drank it all up in no time and I warmed some more to fill their little tummies. When they had had sufficient, we put them on the floor and watched their antics. We had to find names for them and, as the smaller black one began to explore his environment, we could see his boldness increasing by the minute. The little ginger chap, on the other hand, was much more timid and followed a few steps behind. This gave me their names because the black one was definitely the great explorer and became David Livingstone and the ginger one, following on behind, Henry Stanley.

We took them back to their house in the barn and this time they didn't run to hide but explored the area fully. We renewed the food and drink bowls and left them to their exploration while we got on with our chores. We never had to feed them again and they ate and drank what we provided in the barn and began to grow. They raced around the enclosure and jumped up on the straw and played fighting games together, and then they crashed out in the clothes basket and slept.

After a few days, Richard made a small opening at one corner of their pen and, true to his name, David was the first to peep out at this extension to their world. First of all he peeped, and then he took a few steps before running back to safety. The month was May and the cows were coming in each day for their feed and soon David was joining them in their section of the shed. He raced in and out of their legs without any fear and then ran back to his pen. Henry took much longer to venture forth.

Soon David was spending much of his time exploring the shed and Henry began to follow. When I took their food out to them, David would follow me to the shed door and watch me go back into the house. It wasn't long before he was following me across the yard with Henry in his wake, and when we left the door open in the warm summer weather, of course they made their way inside and found the warm spot by the old Esse range. This was the end of Richard's rule that they were not to be house cats and has become their routine. Most mornings they appear at the back door as soon as they hear us moving about in the house and they spend most of the colder days in the kitchen sleeping and go out on patrol at night. They have both become excellent hunters and have fulfilled their role as rodent operatives wonderfully.

When I arrived back from the hospital, they were both there to meet me as usual and I scooped Henry up and buried my tear stained face in his soft fur. They came in with me and settled themselves in the kitchen while I went to the telephone. I had decided on the drive home that my best plan was to seek the aid of John Finlay at Blackcraig in finding a home for the cattle, as he would know of any avenues that might be open. I rang and told him of our plight and asked him what the best way to go about selling the cattle, or even if he could do it for me. His answer brought on a fresh bout of tears because it was the very last thing that I was expecting. 'No' he said, 'I will not sell your cows. It is not a good time to sell cows with small calves and you will not get good prices. I may be able to get rid of the young steers at a good price and I have a man coming in a day or two to buy Galloway heifers, but Ian and I will come and feed your cows for you until Richard is back on his feet. That way you will be well placed to grow your numbers again as soon as possible.' I didn't know what to say. This was an answer that had never even occurred to me and I doubt if I was able to say very much to John, as he had certainly taken my breath away. He told me to leave things with him and to call him again if he could help in any other way. He would ring again soon.

I got myself something to eat and took a phone call from Roy asking what the news was. When I told him, he said that he would come and do the feeding morning and night on as many days as he could and he would try to make sure that the cows had enough silage for the days he couldn't come, so that John and Ian would only be required occasionally. I knew that I would be able to manage the ration feeding and so life began to take on a much happier feeling. The shock of these two offers was every bit as strong as that I had suffered in the hospital, but was of a totally different kind. I cannot express the depth of gratitude that I felt towards these people who had come to our aid without a second thought, committing themselves to so much extra work for an extended period of time when their own lives were so busy.

When I got back to Richard that afternoon, it was with all this happy news. He had been admitted to a ward and was lying on the bed with his leg in a padded cloth splint fitted with Velcro fastenings. He had not heard when his operation was to be and had no more news about his situation. We talked about the cattle and he said he would leave it to me to decide with John, Ian and Roy what was to be done and I left him in a much better frame of mind to drive home before dark.

Catherine had also rung to say that she couldn't get up to me until the next day but she had taken two days off work and would arrive at 2 p.m. the next afternoon.

Roy came at 4p.m. and sorted out the feeding and, when he left, I closed the drive gate behind him and, leaving David and Henry outside, I went inside and locked all the doors and made preparations to spend my first night alone at Low Arvie.

I have never been very good at spending nights alone, even where there are people around and this was to be a big ordeal for me. Its very strange, but on the nights when we are both at home, Richard can be down the fields maybe with calving cows up to half a mile away until the wee small hours and I never worry about being alone at all, but let him be away from the farm altogether and the dark windows of the kitchen frighten me to death. The curtains I had made for these windows were more for show than use, and the thought of spending the evening imagining that strange faces were going to peer in at me was a definite no. I made myself some kind of a meal and then decamped upstairs to the bedroom and spent the evening up there. I determined to stay awake all night and watch television and then sleep in the morning light before I had to go and collect Catherine from the station and see Richard.

My evening's television was interrupted many times by telephone calls from many people who had heard the news. Anyone who has lived in the country will know that news travels much faster across our empty acres than in the built up regions of towns and cities. I had offers of help from all of them and, once again, I found their concern and kindness overwhelming and tears flowed again, this time of relief, gratitude and happiness. One of the calls was from John to say he had already found a buyer and a good price for our seven yearling steers and that he and Ian would see to rounding them up and loading them into their transport, which was already fixed for Wednesday afternoon. I asked who the buyer was and he said that it was a man from Stranraer with whom he had dealt often and that he would give them a good home.

In between receiving the calls, I rang my cousin Gaye to tell her the news. She is my best friend, apart from Catherine, and she and her husband, Tony, had visited the farm several times. When she had told Tony the news, she rang back and said that they had arranged to come up to Low Arvie on Friday and stay with me till Sunday.

Of course, I didn't stay awake all night and when I awoke safe and sound the next morning and played through in my mind the events of the previous twenty-four hours, I knew how truly lucky we are.

27

Broken leg, Poland and a Funeral

Richard did not have his operation until the Wednesday and the nurses told me that he would be in theatre for a long time and then very groggy afterwards, and so I decided that, as I could not be of any help to him and he would be well looked after, I would take the opportunity to go back to Warwick with Catherine and see Mother who was still recovering from her Christmas Day problem. I did not know when I would be able to get down again and this added to my worries.

Roy was able and willing to see to the cattle and feed David and Henry for the two days I would be away and John assured me that he and Ian didn't require my help with the steers. I gave them the passports which had to accompany the animals and left them to it.

The visit eased my mind about Mother as she was obviously well out of danger now and I explained to her about Richard's leg. I knew that she would not remember unless reminded but Catherine would do this and would give her the explanation if my absence was prolonged.

I came back to Dumfries on Friday with Gaye and Tony and we called in to see the patient on our way to the farm. He had recovered well from the operation and his leg was still in the same splint as before. He had been able to get out of bed and was learning how to use crutches to move about without putting his broken leg to the floor. His recovery progressed normally from this point and he was soon crutching his way around the ward with ease. He is very strong and this helped enormously in the process.

The steers had gone to Stranraer with no trouble in my absence and John rang to say that the man who wanted to buy Galloway heifers would be arriving in the area the next week. I was a bit shocked when he explained that the man was coming from Poland and the heifers were to start a new herd in that country, but John said that he had sent animals abroad and that the transport they used was first class and all the animals had always arrived safely. I think I would have declined the offer if I had had any choice, as the thought of my poor Ladies travelling half way across Europe filled me with dismay. However, I know that the rules for transporting animals are as strict as all the others we have to live by and, having no real other choice, I agreed to the visit. I got out the herd book and looked miserably at the likely candidates. There were the four heifers that were out with Gusto, and the six yearlings. It was very difficult, but I knew it had to be done and in the end I decided to let all the four heifers go. This would reduce the pressure on the silage and would mean that Roy might not have to make so many trips with the trailer. This would leave us with thirteen cows and their ten calves in Eastside with Gusto and the three cows who had been inseminated and whose calves were due in February and March. They were living together in the new shed and the little paddock. I then looked at the list of yearling heifers. There were six of them including Eve Chouette who was not wanted by the Poles because of her Beltie genes. Of the remaining five, there were two that I could not bear to part with. One was Bonnie who is Beauty's calf. Beauty was now ten years old and would not have too many more calves and, as her latest one was a steer, I wanted to keep her blood line on the farm. The other one was Demelza who was Beauty's grand daughter and she was growing into a very fine animal. Even John said he wouldn't mind her in his herd, so I took her name off the selling list. That left three names uncrossed. These were Rosemary, Erica and Zara and reluctantly I decided that these should go. Rebecca and Elizabeth, the mothers of Rosemary and Erica, were still young cows and would have more calves, and Zinnia, the mother of Zara, was rearing another heifer in Eastside and so her bloodline was secure. The next Wednesday John and Ian came and put these seven together into the old shed for the Polish contingent to 'interview' and, when they came I found myself unable to go out with them and left John to do the negotiating. He said that they were delighted with our stock and had agreed to take them all.

It would take a few weeks for all the paperwork to be completed and so they would remain with us for a little while longer. The work load, though, was eased by the sale of the steers and there were now just the cows and calves in Eastside, the three pregnant cows and the ten heifers in the new shed to be fed each day.

I fetched Richard home the day after the Poles had been and, by this time, he was adept at standing on one leg when stationary and at moving about with his crutches. His leg was still splinted but in a new type of splint. It was made of fabric and Velcro like the other one but it was hinged at the knee with a metal hinge so that he could alter the 'angle of bend' and keep the knee joint flexible. When we got back and he had received a warm welcome from David and Henry, he showed me how he had learnt to go upstairs and I soon saw that his strength of mind was going to aid him to carry on as normally as he could. This was proved half an hour later when I found him by the back door with his coat on, fastening a plastic Tesco carrier bag around his still swollen right foot. Heedless of my complaints, he then proceeded to ease himself and his crutches through the door and went off to make an inspection of his domain.

On February 10th, my life was disrupted once more when I received a telephone call from the Manager of the Care home in Doncaster where my Mother's sister, my Auntie Ethel, was living. She had reached her 103rd birthday in December, but I had not been able to visit her since the previous September. She did not recognise me any more, but she had been well, and then I had received a photograph of her taken on her birthday with the flowers I had sent her. Mechele was ringing to tell me that she had had a stroke that morning and had been taken to hospital. There was no way I could leave the farm and Mechele assured me that there was nothing I could do in any case. I made daily phone calls to monitor her progress and the prognosis did not sound to be good. She was taken back to the home after a few days but Mechele thought that this would probably prove to be the end.

Life developed into a new normality. Roy came when he could and saw to the silage, and on the few occasions that he couldn't, Ian filled in. I did the cattle cake feeding and nobody suffered from the lack of care. With hindsight I think we could have probably managed without selling the heifers, but it did afford us some prestige, as this was the first batch of Galloways to go abroad since the Foot and Mouth outbreak had halted exports some seven years previously and the day the lorry came to collect them, we also had a photographer from the local paper to record the event and Richard's picture appeared with the cattle in both the local paper and the national Scottish Farmer.

I must admit I did go and peer into the lorry before the Ladies were loaded and was pleased to find that John had been right when he told me that they would have excellent quarters for their journey. Each had their own space with food and water provided and a comfortable bed. I gave them a copy of 'The Ladies of Low Arvie' to take with them for their new owner, so that he would know about their heritage. They left us on a Wednesday and the next Saturday afternoon I received an email from them saying they had all arrived safely and they had even attached photographs of themselves disembarking from the lorry and getting their first views of their new home. We have continued to receive emails and photographs and have been able to follow their progress. Two of the older heifers were in calf to Gusto and now they have just had their second calf. Their new owner, Simon, visits the UK from time to time and tells us he is delighted with them. There is even a possibility of us visiting them in Poland in the not too distant future!

Richard was now progressing well and the only thing he really struggled to achieve was washing his hair, but he said he would be able to manage on his own and that I should make my planned trip to Warwick on February 20th to see Mother and to fit in some studying time. My journeys south have to be arranged about two months in advance in order to purchase the much cheaper Advance tickets. When emergencies occur, I sometimes have to cancel the trips, or purchase full price tickets, but it was still cost effective to try and plan so far ahead and the tickets for this trip were bought before the accident. From Warwick, it would also be easier for me to go to Doncaster and visit Auntie Ethel because I keep my little car at the apartment and the journey to Doncaster by car is less than two hours. I was at Carlisle station waiting for my train to Leamington, when Mechele rang me to say that Ethel had died peacefully during the previous night. I felt sad, but in another way I felt that she had had a good long life which had come to its end in as easy a way as possible as she had remained unconscious since her stroke. I continued on my journey south and then spent the next day driving to Doncaster to collect her effects, getting the death certificate and registering the death, before going to see the funeral director and arranging for her burial on February 29th.

By this time, I was back home and Richard and I drove down to Doncaster and met up with my brother for the church service in the parish church at Conisborough where she had worshipped. I did not expect many people to be at the church because she had been in the Care Home for more than ten years and so I was very touched that about twenty people turned out to pay their respects to her and made the service a worthy send off for a lady of such a great age. Then Richard, Philip and I accompanied her on her last journey to be buried with her first husband in Doncaster.

While I was down in Warwick, Jill had given birth to her Beltie calf, a heifer we named Jeannie after the lady who used to live at Low Arvie. We are not too impressed with the dominance of the Beltie gene as, of the five Beltie calves that have been born on Low Arvie, only Eve Chouette has the full belt and we have now given up the experiment and have reverted to using a Black Galloway bull for any inseminations that are required. Jeannie's belt runs from half way up one flank to the same height on the other and is at least symmetrical but her back is completely black.

The heifers had departed for their new life in Poland when we kept Richard's appointment at the hospital at the end of March, and the broken leg was X-rayed to see how it was progressing. The consultant was extremely pleased as he could see that the tibia was mending exactly in position and that all being well the femur should be able to make the joint without grating on any small projections at the site of the fracture. He still requested that Richard should keep his weight off the leg until his next appointment in four weeks time.

On this next visit to the hospital, we did not see the consultant, but one of his staff. This man allowed us to see the X-ray and Richard had his first view of the damage the kick had caused. We could plainly see the fracture sight and the metal plate with six two-inch screws holding it in place inside his leg. We were surprised when the doctor said that the break was now completely healed and that Richard could throw his crutches away and use the leg normally, just resting it if he felt he needed to. We explained about the heavy nature of farm work, carrying large sacks etc. but the doctor did not seem at all concerned about this and still insisted that he should carry on as normal. What did Richard do? There and then he put his right foot to the ground and lifted his left, so that his leg had gone from carrying no weight to carrying all of it in a split second. I could not think that this was a good thing.

However, we did as the doctor said and Richard began to catch up with the less important tasks that had been put on hold over the previous weeks. On the next day he climbed the ladder to the water tanks in the cattle shed and readjusted the float switches that allowed the water to refill the tanks from the well. He also began to do the silage, which entails climbing up and down on the trailer yanking the plastic jacket and the net wrapping off the bales.

I was down in Warwick the next week, when on one of our long phone calls, he told me that he had got concerned about his leg and had rung the consultant. I think he must have been horrified that Richard was using his leg normally only ten weeks after the accident and he told Richard to take all his weight off it again, go back to using the crutches and to present himself at the hospital the next morning. Happily the X-ray showed that no damage had been done in the ten days of normal use, but the consultant said the Richard should continue to protect the leg by using the crutches for four more weeks and he arranged for him to have physiotherapy at the cottage hospital in Castle Douglas.

After this, things progressed well and Richard was able to get back to using his leg properly again by the time June came. He obviously doesn't have as much power in the limb as he used to and he has had to stop racing around so much but, by and large, his leg is almost as good as new. The only worry left is that the consultant was positive that he will develop arthritis over the next few years, and he will require a new knee joint at some point in the future. Before this can be done, the metal plate and screws have to be removed and then there has to be at least a year's interlude before the joint can be replaced to allow the screw holes in the bones to fill in and strengthen. Hopefully, this will not be for some time yet!

28

Ermintrude interlude

After the departure of the heifers, we had opened up the old shed and the area between that and the new shed for the three inseminated cows and the new calf, Jeannie, to give them a bit more room. Our oldest cow, Emerald, was the next one due to calve and we kept a look out for signs that this was imminent.

We had gone to bed early to watch an episode of Taggart on the evening of March 12ᵗʰ and above the noise of the television we could hear one of the cows mooing loudly. At first we did not take too much notice as this often occurs when a cow cannot find her calf and we continued to watch the programme. After some time, the mooing seemed to get louder and more urgent and Richard got up and opened the window to see which direction the sound was coming from. It was Jill and we could not think that she had lost her calf in the darkness because their area was small compared to Eastside where the other cows with calves were. The noise grew louder and louder and then we began to hear the sounds of cows crashing into gates interspersed with the moos. There was nothing for it but to go and see what the problem was.

I had noticed that Jeannie had been spending a lot of time lying near to Emerald for the past two days and, when we got outside, we saw that Emerald had begun to calve and the beginnings of the calf's protective membranes were dangling from her rear end, but, being in her dotage, she thought that Jeannie was her calf and she was refusing to let Jill anywhere near her. The two cows were rushing round crashing into the gates and barging each other about, with little Jeannie between them. Jill was now bellowing her fury as Emerald trapped Jeannie in the corner by the gate and was fending off all Jill's attempts to get at her calf. We stood and watched the pantomime in amazement and Richard crutched his way into the enclosure and stood leaning on the gate wondering what to do. The only thing I could think of was to find help to sort out the problem, as it was plain that Richard could do little and there was no way I was going anywhere near the two angry animals.

It was still only just after 9p.m. and I went back into the house and dialled John Finlay's number. Thankfully he answered and when I had apologised for disturbing him, I explained our problem. He said that he had known this to happen occasionally and promised to come to Low Arvie straightaway. By the time I got back outside Richard had managed somehow to close the gates across the yard and now Jill was on one side, but Jeannie was on the other side with Emerald. Whilst this had calmed down Emerald a bit, Jill was still snorting, pawing the ground and rushing about on her side and I prayed that John would not be long.

In a short while I saw his Defender's lights coming along the road and John and Ian drove into the yard and got out to make a quick assessment of the situation. We explained which cow belonged to the calf and in no time at all John had marched up to Emerald and turned her away from Jeannie. She must have recognised his Galloway authority as she quietly walked into the new shed at his bidding. We shut her in and allowed Jeannie to go back to her mother. The two animals marched off together into the darkness and peace was restored.

John and Ian then went into Emerald and put her into the crush. John said that her own calf was well on its way and he sent Ian back to Blackcraig to fetch their calving jack while we got our breath back and chatted. John is a lovely man who has a ready laugh and our chat was the perfect relaxation that we needed after the worries of the previous half hour. He teased us unmercifully because we had used Beltie semen to inseminate the cows and he is a pure Black man! Ian soon reappeared with the jack. This is a fearsome looking instrument which is attached to the calf in some way and then there is a ratchet mechanism which is operated to bring the calf slowly into the world. I cannot be more specific about how it works as my squeamishness has never allowed me to get too close to the operation, but very soon the two men had Emerald's calf lying in the shed. I fetched the two ear tags and John put them in before letting Emerald out of the crush to tend her new baby. It was a heifer calf and in keeping with our policy of using names with the same initial as the mother, I named her Ermintrude after the cow in The Magic Roundabout. We could see the signs of her Beltie heritage displayed in a large white splodge on one side and a smaller one on the other. There was no further problem with Emerald who seemed as pleased as punch with the newcomer and after watching them bond for a few minutes, John and Ian returned home and we went back to bed. Taggart was just finishing and it seemed amazing that we had only been gone a little under an hour!

29

Intruders

In all the seven years we have lived at Low Arvie, apart from the time Richard was in hospital, I have never felt frightened by its lonely situation in the countryside. To the west our nearest neighbours are about half a mile along the road and to the east there is about three quarters of a mile of fields and woodland separating us and the next house. I confess to some nervousness when Richard is away from the farm late at night, but, by and large, I feel safer there than in the built up areas in which I used to live. However, there have been two occasions when unwelcome visitors have called at the farm.

One summer evening, on one of my earliest visits to Warwick, Richard had gone to bed early with one of his many migraine headaches when he heard footsteps crunching on the stones in the yard. On getting up and looking through the bathroom window, he saw a man leaning over the gate of the old byre taking photographs and Heinz and Yoghurt. Before Richard could dress and confront the man, he had walked off down the drive and, after investigating the area, the only sign of unknown life that Richard could find was a camper van parked at the entrance to the forestry land up past Dot and Willie's farm. There was no one near the van and Richard wrote down the details and then took his headache back to bed.

Feeling better the next day he decided to ring the local police and report the happening to them. The explanation that came from their enquiries settled our minds as to its innocence. The camper van belonged to a man from England who had a son living in sheltered care in Dumfries. Periodically the man comes up and takes his son away on short camping trips in the area. On the occasion that we were investigating the man had brought his son a new camera and he had walked around the vicinity trying out his new acquisition. How or why he found his way up our drive and what the interest was in photographing our two boys, we never found out, nor how he managed to disappear so quickly along our road, but the police assured us that the man had meant no harm and the incident was soon put to the back of our minds.

The only other unwelcome intrusion onto our property occurred in the summer of 2008, when Richard was fully restored to walking on his two legs. The price of diesel had risen sharply and we knew that there were thieves about emptying farm diesel tanks, and sometimes having taken their fill, they left the pipe on the ground allowing the remaining diesel to run away, not only wasting the fuel but leaving the farmer an awful mess to clear up. Some time before, we had moved our diesel tank from the end of the drive out of our sight round the corner of the cattle shed into Eastside field, to clear the view from the new kitchen window but, although now protected behind two gates, it was still visible from the road. The tank is raised up on a wall about six feet high and both the hose pipe from it and the entrance through which the tanker fills it are secured with padlocks. As an extra precaution we fitted an infra red ray at the drive gate to warn us of approaching bodies and vehicles.

Nevertheless, early one morning, Richard was woken, possibly by the ping pong of the infra red device, to hear wheels crunching on the stones out side the bedroom window and creeping out of bed he saw the rear end of a Landrover pickup disappearing around the corner of the cattle shed towards the oil tank. It was still dark and, unable to see the numbers on the bedside phone and unaware of the pimple that all phones have on the number 5 button to allow one to locate all the numbers in the darkness, he went down to the office and phoned the police. Once again, our country situation did not prevent a swift response to his call and within ten minutes a motorway police car that had been called into service in the area from its usual patrol area on the M74 was roaring up the drive. By this time I had woken and the light was beginning to show in the sky. We were hopeful that the thieves were still by the tank, as there had been no sign of them leaving since Richard had returned upstairs and I had woken.

Richard had dressed in the meantime and I put on my dressing gown and we rushed downstairs to point the two policemen in the right direction. Unfortunately the thieves, having put the ladder up to the tank and discovering the padlocks, must have decided that the fast approaching dawn would leave them exposed to view and, while Richard was still unsighted in the office, must have turned around and driven away, for the only signs of their visit were the ladder leaning against the tank, tyre tracks into the field and the open gates. Happily the cattle usually spend the summer nights away from the buildings and we could see them still away down the field.

It was disappointing that we had not been able to catch the thieves red handed and I am not sure that it would have made any difference if Richard had woken me and I had used my knowledge of the pimple on the phone to call the police more quickly. It did, however make for a day that was out of the ordinary at Low Arvie, because having assured themselves that there was nobody to arrest, the motorway policemen left to go back on patrol and we were visited later in the day by the local police, who came to take statements. Later still two very nice scene-of-crimes ladies came and took photographs of the tyre tracks and fingerprint the tank.

We read later in the paper that these thieves had made their way right across Dumfries and Galloway that night, stealing one vehicle and driving on before dumping that one and stealing another. The final vehicle they had stolen belonged to a farmer not far from us and finding oil cans in the back of the pick up, they obviously decided to try and fill them from our tank on their way to Dumfries. They were caught and dealt with, and the incident made us even more security conscious and now we padlock both the drive gate and that into the field every night.

30

Missing from Home!

Throughout all our trials and tribulations of the previous months, I was managing to carry on with my project course, although I cannot say that I was enjoying it very much. I had decided to research the disease Bluetongue that was devastating the animals on the farms of Europe and which had come to England in the late summer of 2007 in midges blown across the channel. The subject matter was interesting and of great importance to us at Low Arvie, because it is a devastating disease for both sheep and cattle and was causing the infected animals much suffering and costing their owners a lot of money and, in some cases, even their business. I used my research to discover and then source and buy the only pour-on product that would help to protect our cows. Scientists in the south of England were working as quickly as possible to create a vaccine but this was not expected to be available until the early part of 2009. Until then, all we could do was to use this pour-on liquid, which effectively turned the cows into walking midge killers, but it was not clear whether the midge died before its bite could inject the Bluetongue virus into the cow's bloodstream. The virus was spread by infected midges biting uninfected animals and then it multiplied in the animal and was passed on in their blood to other midges. It was a clever little beastie and I found this scientific research as interesting as I had the Cryptosporidiosis study. The part of the project that I was not enjoying was the half of it that was concerned with ethical issues, but I struggled on and tried to make a good job of it.

My final two courses were to be the two practical courses scheduled to be held in Nottingham in July and August We had contacted John and Suzie and they were to come and farm sit during the second week of our absence and our friends Maurice and Pauline had agreed to come for the first one in July. This course was the Molecular Basis of Disease and we were to study DNA 'fingerprinting'. I was really looking forward to this, because Catherine studied this technique in the early days of its use when she was at University in 1994 and I had been very interested in her studies then. The second course was to study the process of photosynthesis in which green plants use the sun's light to turn carbon dioxide into the carbohydrates we eat, and, in the process, produce the oxygen that has allowed life to develop on the earth.

To gain my dream of a First Class degree, I would need to gain Distinctions in all three of these courses and I knew that this was not possible. Even if the practical courses went without a hitch and I did well in those, there was no way that the Bluetongue project would be good enough, and I reconciled myself to gaining a good Upper Second class degree and came to think that this would be something to be quite proud of at my advanced years. The one missing mark in the Latin exam was still on my mind but I was now determined to finish as well as I could.

The week before we were due to leave for Nottingham, I opened the door in the morning to find only David waiting to come in. I was not worried because this was the summer and sometimes the night's hunting stretched into the daylight hours, but when Henry was still missing that afternoon at feeding time, I knew that something was wrong. He had never missed feeding time in all his five years. Ever since that first morning when I had fed Henry and Richard had fed David, the cats had remained loyal to the hand that gave them that first drink of milk. When we sit down after lunch, Henry always prefers my lap and David jumps up and snuggles down with Richard, and so I felt the loss very keenly. We began to search the farm calling Henry and, whereas he would usually appear from somewhere, this time there was no sign of him. We extended the search area down the fields and, when Henry still did not appear, we got in the car and drove along the road. We called at the few houses and one lady told us that she had seen a ginger cat in a field about five miles away. We drove on and stopped along the way calling Henry's name but found no trace. I was utterly heart broken, and although Richard doesn't show his emotions, I know that he felt the same. In the following days, I continued the search, driving up and down the road in any spare moments. Richard took a stick and searched the overgrown roadsides and even went over the wall into the wood, wondering if he had been hit by a car and had crawled away into the undergrowth or had been thrown over the wall. I rang the local radio station who report missing animals to a wider audience and I posted his details on the Missing Pets website on the Internet. All to no avail!

The day of our leaving came and we left the farm in the hands of Maurice and Pauline and drove down to Nottingham to investigate DNA.

In the nine days that Henry had been missing, I had slowly accepted that he was gone. There was no reason I could think of why he should have wandered away from our 120 acres which was the only home he had known and I was convinced that he was lying dead somewhere, poisoned or run over. To have found his body would have given me some consolation, but the not knowing was very hard to bear.

The course at Nottingham was so interesting that it served to take away some of the sadness and I enjoyed the practical work very much. We were researching genetic variation and learning how some people have genes that make them more susceptible to developing disease, in our case the disease HIV, whilst others have more protective genes. Even though this was only the nursery slopes of genetic science, it was extremely interesting and enlightening and it made me wish that I was eighteen again and could take up genetic research as a career. The whole experience of my Biological studies with the OU made me envious of those students young enough to continue on to further work and it confirmed what I had long since suspected: that I should have studied science at 'A' level instead of the languages I had chosen. I did not regret my career in teaching and had thoroughly enjoyed it, but I could not stop myself from wondering what might have been.

It was not till the Wednesday that I found a message on my mobile asking me to ring home. Pauline had received a call from someone wanting to come for Bed and Breakfast and she needed to know if we would be available for the required dates. As an after thought at the end of this call she said, 'Oh, by the way, your cat's back!' Pauline is not a cat lover and obviously did not appreciate the angst and worry that losing a beloved pet in such circumstances could bring. Apparently Henry had reappeared the previous Sunday and as far as I could judge from her words, he was fit and well.

I could not wait to get home and reassure myself about his condition and, sure enough, he seemed a bit thinner but was well and just the normal Henry. He was obviously pleased to see us back at Low Arvie and has never strayed again.

The only person who did not seem to welcome Henry back into the fold with open arms, or rather paws, has been David. Since that time, the two cats have not been as friendly and David, being the more aggressive of the two, will sometimes attack Henry for no apparent reason when we are otherwise occupied and I find lumps of ginger fur on the carpet and sometimes adhering to David's whiskers. However, they do still lie contentedly together in front of the Aga.

We have never solved the mystery of Henry's absence and, although I often ask him where he went, the only answer I receive is a contented purr.

31

What Summer?

It was that stressful time of year again when we begin to monitor the weather forecasts closely, looking for the requisite dry days to get the silage done. But in 2008 we were watching for all of July and all of August and still the grass was out in the fields, and the rain never let up enough for us to get it mowed. We went to Nottingham for the two courses, Henry went missing and returned and I completed my reports about DNA and Photosynthesis and still the grass was growing. It was well past the optimum time for cutting it and the nutritious sugars that we hoped to harvest would long since have transferred themselves into the seed which the wind by now would have blown away. The grass was almost beginning to die back before we took advantage of a break in the weather in the second week of September and Tom came and cut the fields. We knew that it would be very poor food for the cattle, but it would be better than nothing and, fortunately, our traditional Galloways would manage to fill their stomachs and produce their milk and we could supplement this ropy product with a bit of extra cake ration. It was less good for the more commercial breeds that require higher quality food and farmers all around were voicing their concerns.

It was, therefore, a relief to us when we managed to get all the grass mown and, all but that on the very steepest slopes where the big tractor pulling the baler just could not get any grip on the wet ground, baled, wrapped and collected before once more the rain poured down. We had made double the number of bales that we had the previous year, but they contained only 25% of actual grass and, as this was so wet, the remaining 75 % was water.

The weather also prevented us from following our programme of weaning the previous year's calves and separating the cows for a few weeks before their new calves were born and this worried me very much as the weather stayed wet. The cows and calves were up in Auchenvey field this year and were still altogether when Richard went up on August 11th and discovered that Rebecca had calved during the night. I needn't have worried about the weaning though, as Nature obviously had her own way of dealing with the situation and Rebecca took care of her new calf in the usual way. We called him Rebel for coming so early. Catherine and Zinnia also calved before their old calves were weaned and coped in the same way. Of course, we were only expecting eight calves this year, with the depletion of the herd when Richard broke his leg. Three more were born soon after we got the silage done and moved the cows into the grass fields.

Towards the end of September, there were only three cows left to calve and on one of his early morning inspections, Richard noticed that Lady Olga had a large prolapse showing at her rear end. We assumed that she was about to calve and quickly put her in the shed and called the vet. However, the calf was not ready to appear and the vet suggested that we leave her close to the house and keep an eye on her. He managed to push the prolapsed vagina a little way back towards its normal internal position but it could be clearly seen bulging out when she lay down.

On the 6th October I went to my usual Friday morning Latin group where half a dozen of us gather to have fun and attempt to translate some of the classical writings of that language. This is one of my most favourite occupations and I really enjoy these gatherings. It had begun as a day class, 'Latin for Fun', about three years before and we had continued to meet in Castle Douglas when Dumfries and Galloway Council decided that they would stop all day and evening classes in a bid to save money. Our erstwhile tutor, Cate Murray, had agreed to carry on teaching us in spite of the fact that we sometimes turned into twelve year old boys on the threshold of the class and misbehaved terribly. By this time we had become a close knit group of half a dozen sixty somethings who had actually learned to love Latin in the very dim and distant past and we do our best under Cate's tutelage to recall our learning of those long ago days to struggle through the finer points of Virgil and Ovid. Since I had completed my OU Latin courses, I probably find it easier than the others, but as we are not under any pressure to be perfect, we get along just fine. We are rewarded several times a year with a visit from the internationally known Latin and Greek guru, Dr. Peter Jones, Cate's old university tutor, when he comes to enthral us with aspects of his learning. We sit entranced by his charismatic delivery, even though much of it is somewhat beyond our ken, and we are very grateful to him for giving up his precious time to travel to Castle Douglas so often. We also sometimes appear in the articles he writes for national publications, variously referred to as 'Cate's Dalry Dazzlers', 'Mrs Murray's Too Good to Hurry Classics Group', 'Cate's Mates', 'a feisty classical adult-education group in Castle Douglas' or 'the wonderfully argumentative adult group in Castle Douglas'.

When I returned to Low Arvie that particular afternoon, I found that Richard had discovered the reason for Olga's bulge as she had just given birth to our first set of Galloway twins. Although this was an exciting event, it was tinged with slight disappointment and the twins were one of each sex. When this occurs in cattle, it is almost certain that the female is sterile because some of the hormones of the male calf creep into her system in the womb and prevent her from developing a normal female reproduction system. These animals are called freemartins. Nevertheless, it was a bonus to our low number of expected calves which rose from eight to nine.

However, this reverted back to eight when we lost our first Low Arvie born calf a few days later. Dorothy struggled to give birth to her calf and, when he was born, it was clear that all was not well. He was a large calf and we had to get the vet out to help, but the umbilical chord must have broken before the calf could get into the air and begin breathing properly. He was very floppy and showed no inclination to suckle or behave normally. In spite of our best efforts and those of the vet, the poor little chap only lived for two days before giving up the fight for life. He was the 96th Low Arvie calf and we felt we had done well to rear almost 99% of our progeny, but it was still a sad day when he died.

One day about this time, we received a letter from Range Rover, recalling our model for the exchange of a part that had proved faulty and it said that the work would take a whole day to complete and we would be given a replacement vehicle while this was being done. We had to take the car to the garage at Carlisle and so we arranged with them to go on a day when the replacement vehicle was available. This vehicle was to be the very latest top of the range model and we decided to take advantage of this opportunity to have a day out as well as to test drive the new vehicle. It seemed the perfect opportunity to fulfil our promise and carry on from Carlisle to Kelso in the borders and visit our Ladies who had been sold to Tommy Platt in 2005.

We found them in their new home housed in two fields by the side of a country lane and we discovered that Tommy was just as caring of his charges as we were. They were very comfortable and content and we spent time learning about their lives from Tommy and his wife. We left them to continue their happy relationship and returned to Carlisle in time to pick up our car. We had thoroughly enjoyed our day out in the new Range Rover that even impressed Richard with its handling and driveability.

I managed to finish off the Bluetongue project and heaved a sigh of relief when the required three copies were posted off for marking. I knew that none of the reports were of distinction quality but I was hopeful that they might enable me to achieve the Upper Second class degree that was now my goal. Strangely, instead of the euphoria that I expected to feel at this moment, I found myself quite flat and wondering what I was going to do with the spare time I now had. For the moment, I just carried on with my usual tasks of keeping the farm paper work up to date, going to the Latin group and visiting Mother.

As I hoped, this space left when I finished with the OU gradually began to close. We had a few B&Bers in the autumn and Gaye and Tony came to visit. On one of the day trips to the small, picturesque beach at Mossyard, which Gaye loves to do on their visits, we called in at the Pit Stop Diner in Twynholm, near Kirkcudbright, for a cup of tea. This small village is the home of David Coulthard, the Formula One racing driver and the Pit Stop Diner contains a small museum of his racing memorabilia. Both Richard and Tony are Formula One fans and they enjoyed looking round the museum while

Gaye and I chatted over the teapot. When the men came back, we began talking to the lady in the café and discovered that, on race days, she cooks a brunch meal for the fans who gather there and then everyone watches the race together on the big screen television in the café. This was most interesting to Richard and Tony and they agreed to join the throng of fans on the next race day. They thoroughly enjoyed the experience and this has now become standard practice for Richard throughout the race season. Tony also comes as often as he can to accompany him. Gaye and I treat ourselves to lunch out and enjoy some girly time together.

The results of my OU courses were released in December and I was thrilled to discover that I had achieved Grade 2s in all four of the courses I had done. None of the pass marks were too near to the magic 85% distinction level, but they were comfortably within the Grade 2 zone, including, surprisingly, the mark for the Bluetongue project, and I was awarded my Upper Second class degree. These grades did mean that had I been able to achieve the 1% more in the Latin exam and 6% more in the Infectious disease exam, it would have been my coveted First. Writing this book has put things into a clearer perspective for me and, when I contemplate all the other challenges that we faced during my four years of study, I find that I can be proud of my OU achievement and the depression that these results caused me has passed into history, along with all the other bad emotions that our ups and downs that the past five years have brought. All those that remain are healthy and good.

32

End of an Era

Christmas 2008 came and went. This time I spent the festive season in Warwick and returned home to Richard for Hogmanay. We did actually celebrate this year by inviting Roy and his wife Tina, along with Diane and Graham, who had helped the American ladies, to join us for a meal.

It was mid morning on January 5th when Catherine rang to say that Mother had pneumonia and, even before letting us know that she was ill, the staff at Clarendon Manor had sent for an ambulance and she was on her way to Warwick Hospital. Catherine said that it sounded serious and that she was on her way there from work and would ring me with more news when she arrived. I began to make hasty preparations to leave Low Arvie and, when Catherine rang to say that Mother was very ill indeed, Richard took me to Dumfries and I caught the early afternoon train south. While I was travelling, Catherine consulted with the doctor at the hospital and it was agreed that they would give her one course of antibiotics and see what happened. We were adamant that we didn't want any kind of invasive treatment to Mother's frail body and prepared ourselves for what might come.

When I arrived at the hospital, I found Mother conscious but obviously very poorly and about to be taken onto a ward in the hospital. We stayed with her for while until she was settled and then said we would return the next day. It was touch and go for a day or two but then the antibiotics, coupled with the strength of Mother's constitution, worked their magic and she began to shake off the pneumonia once again. Two weeks later she was delivered back to Clarendon Manor to resume her convalescence. However, on her return, the girls there were horrified to find that the hospital had allowed a grade three bedsore to develop at the base of her spine and the district nurses decreed that she had to remain in bed until it healed. The hospital had never breathed a word to any of us about this and we all felt so angry with them. Mother had been incontinent for all of her time at Clarendon and the staff there, who had little training and were not paid well, had kept her skin wholesome for the whole time and I was aghast that trained nurses at the hospital should not have managed to do the same. Furthermore their appalling lack of communication, especially to the staff at Clarendon, was a terrible indictment of our National Health Service.

.I also knew that this was the worst possible thing that could happen to Mother and I pleaded with the district nurses to find some way to allow her to get up and participate more fully in life at the home. Apart from the day or two that she had spent in bed during her bouts of pneumonia at Carlingwark and Clarendon Manor in the last few years, I had only ever known her to take to her bed once in my lifetime. She always preferred to get up and take any necessary rest fully clothed and to remain as active as possible. I feared that the enforced confinement in her room for the two or three months that it would take for the deep sore to heal could not have anything other than the worst of outcomes. But they were adamant, and the Care Home staff could not go against the edict of the district nurses.

As I knew would happen, Mother began to deteriorate in spite of our efforts to keep her cheerful during this enforced imprisonment. The district nurses came every day to dress her wound and it slowly began to improve. Morgan brought a television and fixed it up in her room. I spent as much time as possible in Warwick and Catherine visited as often as she could. Mother still met us each day with the same beaming smile but we watched helplessly as the deterioration continued. On my visit on Thursday February 26th, though, there was no beaming smile, just a frail old lady lying in bed with no sign of recognition and, as I sat and held her hand, I knew in my heart that my worst fears were coming true. I visited again with Catherine on the following three days but found no change and I knew that this really was goodbye.

With Mother now no longer responding to my visits, I felt that I should go home and give my attention to Richard and the farm. He had been so supportive throughout these weeks, when the most arduous work at the farm had to be done and he had never minded when I hadn't been able to leave his meals prepared for him on my fleeting visits back to Galloway. With a heavy heart, I left Warwick on Monday morning to go back to Low Arvie and Catherine paid her last visit to her grandmother on her way home from work on that Monday evening.

Mother died peacefully in the early hours of Tuesday March 3rd, surrounded by the love and care of the night staff at Clarendon Manor. She would have been 97 years old on Easter Sunday, April 12th. I learned that the two carers on duty had sat with her all through the night and had performed the final duties for her with all the respect and love that they had always shown her in life. My gratitude to them knows no bounds.

Mother had two sisters, Ethel and Muriel, and neither of these had had children of their own. We were a close family and, being the only girl in the next generation and the one who lived close, it had been my lot to care for these three ladies and their husbands in their final years. This responsibility had begun for me back in 1987 when Muriel's husband developed cancer and it had continued almost continuously throughout the next twenty-two years. The death of Auntie Ethel the previous year had left Mother as the sole survivor and now all that remained of my duty of care for this generation was to organise her funeral. Catherine and Morgan saw to all the official requirements in Leamington, registering her death and clearing her things from Clarendon.

The last thing I could do for Mother was to give a tribute to her at the funeral and I managed to put my grief to one side and perform this final farewell. She had lived a long and happy life and I had wished for a better way for it to end, but at the back of my mind I knew that, in some ways, it was a blessing that her frail body would cause her no more problems. This book is dedicated to her memory and I reproduce here my final farewell so that my tribute to her will endure.

Mary Tyrrell 1912 – 2009

Mary was born in Conisborough near Doncaster on April 12th 1912 just as the Titanic set sail. She was the daughter of the Coop manager in Conisborough and she went from there to Mexborough Grammar School where she knew my father. The family then moved to Doncaster and she transferred to Doncaster Girl's High School. When she left school after a fairly undistinguished academic career she became an infant teacher in Rossington. One day whilst walking to get the bus to Rossington she was stopped by a young man who said, 'I bet you don't remember me!' and her reply was 'Oh yes I do, you're Tyrrell'. They were married on September 2nd 1939 and the wedding was seriously disrupted by the imminence of war, causing many guests to be unable to attend. The prospective honeymoon to the Lake District was postponed and in fact did not take place until twenty-five years later! The couple moved into the new home they had bought on Melton Road, where they lived together for 58 years until Father's death in 1997. By the time women teachers were recalled to the classroom with the call-up of many men for the war effort, Mother was pregnant and so did not return. She had three children at four yearly intervals and consequently never returned to paid work except for a short stint as a dinner lady at Richmond Hill Infant School. She filled her life with village affairs and bringing up her family. She was the chairman of the Sprotborough Infant School PTA, spent many years as Chairman of the Richmond Hill Townswomen's Guild and was a part of the sewing circle which met every Thursday to embroider tablecloths for the bi-annual Church Sale of Work and, no doubt, to exchange village events. (I hesitate to mention the word gossip!). When Father retired from teaching they became founder members of the village Retired Person's Association – or 'the old folks' as I used to call it. This Association was very successful through many years and together Mother and Father organised countless holidays and day trips for the retired people of Sprotborough. They also made several trips to Canada to see their eldest son and his family and travelled extensively in that country.

When Father became ill two years before he died, she struggled on to make his last years as comfortable as possible, and when he died I felt it was her turn to be looked after. I promised her that I would do just that and we had a happy final trip to Canada the following Christmas. Mother was by this time 85, but her strength returned after Father's death and she was able to forge a new and satisfying life doing all the things she wanted to do, including continuing to worship weekly in this church. She sat in this front pew every Sunday for 63 years.

In 2002 when Richard and I bought a farm and made our plans to go and live in beautiful Galloway, Mother had no hesitation in taking up my suggestion that she should come with us and she moved into the sheltered care of the local Abbeyfield home in Castle Douglas where she continued to enjoy her love of reading, doing the Telegraph crossword, worshipping in the lovely church next door and enjoying daily walks to Carlingwark Loch. She spent four very happy years there until life began to be more of a burden and she moved into residential care. When she recovered from a bout of pneumonia in the early spring of 2006 and she became unable to walk far and no longer wanted to travel to England to see other members of the family, we decided that she should move to care in Leamington Spa where they could visit her more easily. Clarendon Manor has remained her home for the rest of her life and we cannot thank the staff there enough for the caring way they have made her last years comfortable and happy.

As my personal tribute to her, I have to say that she has made my chosen task of looking after her in her last years not only easy, but an absolute joy. She had the knack of making all who came into contact with her love her unconditionally. She never complained about anything, and always greeted our every visit with a beautiful beaming smile right to the end. As her health failed in these last two months, Catherine and I have spent many hours sitting with her, sharing her last days with sadness in our hearts but a smile on our lips. We know that she is now at peace and our task is over, but it was never a burden and it was one we would gladly have continued. We shall miss her.

My brother came over from Canada, not as he was planning to do to celebrate her birthday with her, but to help lay her to rest in the quiet Yorkshire graveyard with our father.

33

The Future

For a while after the funeral, my anger at Warwick Hospital would not allow me to grieve and I consulted my brothers and Catherine and we decided to raise a complaint against them. We did not want financial compensation, but to point out to them the consequence of their actions and, hopefully, prevent the same thing happening to other frail, elderly patients. They eventually acknowledged their shortcomings and agreed to institute better training for the staff and better communication with the relevant people.

When this process was over in July, we felt we had done as much as we could and we let the matter rest. We couldn't change what was past and it was time now to move on. Slowly my anger has faded into sadness at Mother's death but I cannot feel sorry that she is now released from the frailty that had overtaken her body in her final years. She did have a long and happy life and we have many good memories to console us

How to move on now is the problem that faces me. My graduation took place in June and I am now entitled to use the letters BSc (Hons.) after my name, but I am probably too old to do anything other than delight in the achievement and dream what might have been if I had done it years ago.

We are gradually building up the numbers of cattle at Low Arvie once again and this autumn there will be twenty-three cows meeting up with

Klondyke Powerhouse in the hope of new calves next year. Richard's leg is as good as it possibly can be and he is able to do all the necessary farm work and maintain the growing array of farm equipment that we have gathered around us. A major improvement has been the purchase of an All-Terrain quad bike which enables him to complete many of the feeding and caring tasks much more quickly, and even I have been known to zoom around the farm on it when necessary.

We plan to carry on with our venture in the same way for at least three more years, when Richard will be sixty-seven, and we will have fulfilled our commitment over the new shed. Then we will take stock of our various abilities and make a decision about the future. If he is still fit and able, we may carry on, or, having fulfilled eleven years of farming at Low Arvie, we may decided to downgrade the work to a method of farming that does not require such hard physical exertions on cold winter days, or even move on to a different life altogether.

We shall keep the flat in Warwick and I continue to make regular trips down to England to spend time with Catherine and Morgan and keep up the friendships, although I shall not go so frequently now that Mother has no more need of my services.

The writing of this book has filled in the gap that opened up for me after my studies finished and Mother's death and now that this oeuvre is finished too, I wait to see what project will take its place.

When my first book was so well received, many people asked when the second one would be available. My answer was always the same. The first twenty months of our farming life created such a complete story in itself that I didn't think there would be anything else to write about that could be as interesting and readable. However, I seem to have found enough material to comply with these requests and maybe the next three years will provide a similar amount of stories too. Who knows?

Certainly not me!